Oxford School *Shakespeare*

THE MERCHANT *of* VENICE

edited by
Roma Gill, OBE
M.A. *Cantab.*, B. Litt. *Oxon*

OXFORD
UNIVERSITY PRESS
Great Clarendon Street, Oxford OX2 6DP

Oxford University Press is a department of the University of Oxford. It furthers the University's objective of excellence in research, scholarship, and education by publishing worldwide in

Oxford New York

Athens Auckland Bangkok Bogotá Buenos Aires Cape Town Chennai Dar es Salaam Delhi Florence Hong Kong Istanbul Karachi Kolkata Kuala Lumpur Madrid Melbourne Mexico City Mumbai Nairobi Paris São Paulo Singapore Taipei Tokyo Toronto Warsaw

with associated companies in Berlin Ibadan

OXFORD is a registered trade mark of Oxford University Press in the UK and in certain other countries

Schools edition first published 1979
First revised edition published 1992
This second revised edition first published 2001
Trade edition first published 1994
This revised edition first published 2001

ISBN 0 19 832016 7 (Schools edition) 3 5 7 9 10 8 6 4 2
ISBN 0 19 832017 5 (Trade edition) 3 5 7 9 10 8 6 4 2

 For this new edition, the introductory matter, the notes, and the text have been revised and reset, the illustrations have been redrawn, and photographs of stage productions have been included.

Illustrations by Alexy Pendle

All photographs by Donald Cooper (Photostage) with the exception of p.114. Cover shows Antony Sher as Shylock in the Royal Shakespeare Company's 1988 production of *The Merchant of Venice.*

Oxford School Shakespeare
edited by Roma Gill

A Midsummer Night's Dream
Romeo and Juliet
As You Like It
Macbeth
Julius Caesar
The Merchant of Venice
Henry IV Part I
Twelfth Night
Much Ado About Nothing
Measure for Measure
The Taming of the Shrew
Othello
Hamlet
King Lear
Henry V
The Winter's Tale
Antony and Cleopatra
The Tempest
Richard II
Coriolanus
Love's Labour's Lost

Typeset by Herb Bowes Graphics, Oxford
Printed in Great Britain by Alden Press Limited

Contents

Introduction

About the Play

A pound of flesh. You know the expression, meaning 'the full and exact repayment of some debt or duty'? It's part of the English language, and the common property of people all over the world who have never heard of *The Merchant of Venice*. But this is where it began.

The play is all about money—and as soon as you say that word the clichés come tumbling out. It's not the most important thing in life, won't bring you happiness, can't buy me love, and is (a common misquotation[1]) the root of all evil. For Portia, who has lots of it, wealth is almost an embarrassment and certainly an obstacle when it comes to finding a husband. For Shylock (who loses his daughter but laments more loudly about the ducats—Venetian gold coins—that she has stolen from him), money still means less than the opportunity to be revenged on his rival. And at the beginning of the play Antonio, a prince among Venetian merchants and a successful dealer in sumptuous luxury goods, is unspeakably and unaccountably depressed. Only Bassanio, broke and reckless, is reasonably cheerful: he has a plan, and just needs funding. His crazy idea—shoot another arrow in the direction of the one you've lost and you'll find both—triggers off the action, and sets both of the play's main plots in motion.

Bassanio can be sure of a loan from his affectionate friend Antonio, but Antonio's money is all tied up in his business ventures, and he must turn to Shylock, a professional moneylender, who demands an unusual security for the loan—a pound of Antonio's flesh.

Shylock is a Jew, a member of a race feared and despised by the Elizabethans for reasons that are complex and historical, and only partly religious. The Jews were hated for their biblical role in the crucifixion of Jesus, certainly, and European countries from the twelfth century had used this pretext for expelling them from their shores. Those who remained were often forbidden to own property, or to engage in any of the professions, and were thereby forced into the business of usury—lending money for profit. And mercantile societies need moneylenders. Some Jews prospered, and their success intensified the distrust of the native English, but Queen Elizabeth numbered a

[1] 'for *the love of money* is the root of all evil', 1 Timothy 6:10.

Jewish woman among her ladies-in-waiting, and even, for a time, had a Jewish doctor as her private physician—although Dr Lopez was eventually (in 1594) charged with trying to poison her, and executed.

All through the play we are aware of anti-Semitic prejudice in many of the characters, but Shakespeare himself takes no sides. His plot, based on a narrative fiction, demanded a Jewish villain—but Shakespeare understood the human suffering that had for centuries been subject to humiliating discrimination, and he allows Shylock to speak for all persecuted minorities:

> Hath not a Jew eyes? Hath not a Jew hands, organs, dimensions, senses, affections, passions? Fed with the same food, hurt with the same weapons, subject to the same diseases, healed by the same means, warmed and cooled by the same winter and summer as a Christian is? If you prick us, do we not bleed?

If we can appreciate this argument, then it is hard not to assent to its logical extension—

> And if you injure us, shall we not revenge?

Antonio is in serious danger when the underdog tries to seize his opportunity for triumph—but this is a comedy, and the good fairy comes to his rescue in the person of Portia, the first of Shakespeare's truly great female roles.

Most modern girls would find Portia's situation intolerable: a wealthy heiress, she is bound to obey the wishes of her deceased father and submit to the test he has devised to choose a husband for her—though not without showing a shadow of resentment that 'the will of a living daughter [should be] curbed by the will of a dead father'. She can only be a daughter of her own times, however, never questioning a man's right to the ownership of all his wife's possessions, and resigning herself happily into the protection of Bassanio—who has won the lottery:

> But now, I was the lord
> Of this fair mansion, master of my servants,
> Queen o'er myself; and even now, but now,
> This house, these servants, and this same myself
> Are yours, my lord's.

Only for the past hundred years or so has a woman in England been allowed to keep her own property after marriage—and sexual discrimination is by no means ended yet.

The *Merchant of Venice* deals with topics and social issues that belong as much, or even more, to the twenty-first century than they did to Shakespeare's own day—fathers and daughters, racial discrimination, colour prejudice, love and friendship. And to all of these there is some financial aspect. Altered attitudes in the twentieth century shifted the emphasis of Shakespeare's play so that it nearly became the *tragedy* of 'The Jew of Venice' (always an alternative title), but the magic of the final Act is powerful. The serious issues and complex figures of the trial scene dissolve into the moonlit serenity of Belmont, and laughter returns the characters and the audience to the real world with Gratiano's final bawdy joke.

Leading Characters in the Play

Antonio The merchant of the play's title. He is a good and generous man, who promises to pay Shylock the money borrowed by Bassanio or else allow Shylock to cut off a pound of his flesh. His part in the play is rather a passive one, and he reveals his character mainly in his generosity to his friend and in his hatred of the Jew.

Bassanio A young man who has already spent all his own money and now hopes to restore his fortunes by marrying an heiress. He needs to borrow money so that he can make a fine display when he courts Portia, and it is for his sake that Antonio enters into the bond with Shylock. Bassanio shows good judgement in his choice of caskets, and wins Portia for his wife.

Gratiano A young man with a reputation for wild behaviour. He accompanies Bassanio to Belmont, and wins the love of Portia's lady-in-waiting, Nerissa.

Lorenzo He is in love with Jessica, the Jew's daughter, and plans to steal her from her father's house.

Portia The most important character in the play. She is an heiress, and is in love with Bassanio; but her father has devised a test with three caskets, and Portia must marry the man who chooses the right casket. Portia is intelligent as well as beautiful; dressed as a lawyer she goes to Venice and saves Antonio from being killed by Shylock. Her home is Belmont, and the peace and harmony here contrast with the tense business world of Venice.

Nerissa Portia's lady-in-waiting, who falls in love with Gratiano. When Portia goes to Venice as a lawyer, Nerissa accompanies her, dressed as a lawyer's clerk.

Shylock A money-lender, who is hated for his greed and because he is a Jew. He is Antonio's enemy, and when Bassanio's money is not repaid he demands the pound of flesh that Antonio promised as a forfeit.

Jessica Shylock's daughter; she disguises herself as a boy in order to run away from her father's house, where she is unhappy. She is in love with the Christian Lorenzo.

Lancelot Gobbo The comedian of the play. He is at first Shylock's servant, then goes to work for Bassanio. His clowning often takes the form of misusing the English language; it is sometimes a welcome break from the tense or romantic scenes.

Synopsis

Act 1

Scene 1 Antonio is very depressed; he is willing to provide funds for Bassanio's expedition to Belmont, but must try to borrow money from Shylock.

Scene 2 Portia longs to find a husband, but all her suitors must submit to a test devised by her father before his death.

Scene 3 Shylock agrees to lend money to Antonio—but he demands an unusual bond.

Act 2

Scene 1 Portia interviews a new suitor, the Prince of Morocco, and explains the terms of her father's will.

Scene 2 Lancelot Gobbo wants to leave Shylock, his master, and find employment with Bassanio, who is preparing for Belmont.

Scene 3 Lancelot says goodbye to Jessica, Shylock's daughter, who gives him a letter for Lorenzo.

Scene 4 Lorenzo is planning some late-night entertainment when Lancelot brings Jessica's letter.

Scene 5 Shylock leaves Jessica in charge of his house.

Scene 6 Lorenzo and his friends rescue Jessica from her father's house.

Scene 7 The Prince of Morocco examines the caskets and makes his choice.

Scene 8 Salarino and Solanio gossip about the news: Lorenzo is missing, Shylock has been robbed, and Antonio is in trouble.

Scene 9 Another suitor makes his choice—and Portia learns that Bassanio is coming to Belmont.

Act 3

Scene 1 Trouble for Antonio: Shylock rejoices in his power over the merchant—and laments for the loss of his daughter.

Scene 2 Bassanio makes his choice of caskets, winning Portia for his wife. Nerissa agrees to marry Gratiano, and both contracts are sealed with a ring. Lorenzo and Jessica arrive in Belmont, bringing a letter from Antonio.

Scene 3 Antonio has been arrested and Shylock threatens him.

Scene 4 Portia and Nerissa plan a visit to Venice.

Scene 5 Lancelot teases Jessica.

Act 4

Scene 1 The trial. Antonio is prepared to die when Shylock refuses to show mercy, but Portia, disguised as a young lawyer, tricks Shylock out of his bond and asks Bassanio for his ring as a reward.

Scene 2 Portia gets Bassanio's ring—and Nerissa plans to get her own from Gratiano.

Act 5

Scene 1 Lorenzo teases Jessica as they wait in the moonlight. Portia and Nerissa return from Venice, followed by Bassanio and Gratiano—who are embarrassed when their wives demand to see the rings. All is explained, and Portia has good news for Antonio.

The Merchant of Venice: commentary

The action of the play takes place in Venice and in Belmont. Belmont is imaginary, but Venice is real. The city is located on the sea coast in the north of Italy, and is in fact built over a lagoon. Its main streets are canals, and the only vehicles are boats (see illustration page 40). In the sixteenth century, Venice was the centre for international trade, importing goods from all corners of the earth, and exporting them in the same way. We are told that Antonio, the greatest of the merchants, is waiting for his ships to return

> From Tripolis, from Mexico, and England,
> From Lisbon, Barbary, and India. (3, 2, 266–7)

To be successful, a merchant had to invest his money wisely—and have luck on his side. Trading by sea was hazardous, and a sudden storm, or unseen rocks, could easily wreck a ship and drown the merchant's hopes along with the cargo.

Act 1

Scene 1 When his friends see that Antonio is depressed, they immediately think that he is worried about his ships at sea. They are sympathetic, and Solanio does his best to make light of the situation by exaggerating his fears to make his friend smile. But Antonio is sad for some other reason, and when we meet his dearest friend, Bassanio, we begin to guess at this reason. Bassanio is a carefree young man, who cheerfully admits that he has spent all of his own money and a good deal of Antonio's. However, Bassanio now has a scheme for acquiring more wealth. Before he gives any details, he explains his theory: a lost arrow (he says) can often be found by shooting another arrow in the same direction, and watching carefully to see where it falls. The theory is, as Bassanio acknowledges, a 'childhood proof'; he believed it when he was a schoolboy, and now he wants to put it to the test again, spending more money in the hope of winning back what he has lost. This is not a very sensible, or responsible, way to act, but Bassanio emphasizes his youth and innocence. Perhaps he hopes that Antonio will treat him as though he were a child, and ignore the irresponsibility of his demand for more money to spend.

Bassanio next tells Antonio of an heiress, who has already given him some unspoken encouragement. Her name is Portia, and Bassanio claims to have fallen in love with her. He may be speaking the truth, but it is clear that the lady's wealth is a very attractive feature for him. Antonio promises aid, but all the money he possesses is tied up in his own business ventures. Still, his 'credit' is good, and Bassanio can borrow all the ducats he needs to present himself to Portia as an eligible suitor, giving Antonio's name as security—that is, promising that Antonio will repay the debt if he himself is unable to do so.

Our feelings towards Bassanio at the end of this scene cannot be wholly favourable, despite his youthful optimism. He has wasted a lot of money, both his own and his friend's. It seems that he wants to marry Portia not just for love, but also for her money. But he himself, perhaps unconsciously, shows what we should feel about him when he explains that his youth has been 'something too prodigal'. Repeated phrases throughout the play compare Bassanio with the Prodigal Son of Christ's parable (St Luke 15:11–32), who spent all his inheritance in 'riotous living'. When he was penniless and starving, he went repentantly back to his father's house, where he was welcomed with rejoicing. Bassanio has been 'prodigal'; now he asks for a chance to redeem himself.

Like the Prodigal Son's father, Antonio has shown the loving and forgiving generosity of his nature, but he remains a mysterious character. Early in the scene he tells Gratiano that he thinks of the world as 'A stage where every man must play a part, And mine a sad one'. It is his changing relationship with Bassanio that causes his melancholy. Some Elizabethans thought—as the Greeks and Romans did—that the friendship between two men was a more spiritual bond, and should be more highly esteemed, than the love between a man and a woman. Knowing that Bassanio is interested in a lady (see lines 119–21), Antonio may be secretly grieving for the inevitable end to a friendship.

Scene 2 From the hearty, but anxious, masculine world of Venice, we move to the feminine peace of Belmont. Even here there is anxiety, as Portia's opening sigh indicates. It is now Nerissa who tries to cheer Portia, but she cannot take her mistress's mind off the situation where she is surrounded by suitors and yet 'cannot choose one, nor refuse none'. Shakespeare has to communicate to his audience a lot of information about the test that Portia's father devised for the men who wish to marry her. The information is given gradually, in five separate scenes, so that we seem to discover the facts just as the suitors do. For the moment, we are merely told that each candidate must make a choice between three caskets.

Nerissa explains why Portia must obey this somewhat absurd commandment when she says that 'holy men at their death have good inspirations'. It was proverbially believed that a good man would be divinely inspired, and might even speak prophetically, when he was close to death. To disobey or disregard such an utterance was almost sacrilege.

The two young women amuse themselves by gossiping about the suitors who have already assembled at Belmont. Although Portia and Nerissa are Italian, they share a sense of humour which is undoubtedly English. As they laugh about each man's peculiarities, we can learn something of what the Elizabethans thought of their continental neighbours—and also of how they could laugh at themselves. The 'young baron of England' is a caricature of the Englishman abroad, in the twenty-first century as well as in the sixteenth: the English have never been good at speaking foreign languages! Nor is there a 'national dress' for England, such as many other countries possess; the English were always content (it seems) to imitate the costumes of other countries. The joke about the Scottish lord would have a topical significance for Shakespeare's audience. At this time England and Scotland were separate kingdoms, and in their frequent quarrels the French always promised to aid the Scots (but rarely kept their promises).

We are never allowed to see this 'parcel of wooers', for Nerissa tells Portia that they have all decided to return home, not trying their luck with the caskets. There is no doubt that Portia is glad they are leaving. Nerissa reminds her of a young Venetian whom Portia met whilst her father was alive, and the promptness with which Portia recalls Bassanio's name is enough to tell us that she remembers him with pleasure. Bassanio is described by Nerissa as 'a scholar and a soldier'. These qualities made up the ideal courtier in Elizabethan eyes, and the description may help to prepare us for a Bassanio who is rather different from the one we left in Venice.

Portia's enthusiasm dies away, and her weary resignation returns, when she is told that a new suitor is approaching Belmont. It is the Prince of Morocco, and the title arouses her prejudice as she goes inside to prepare for his coming.

Scene 3 Meanwhile, in Venice, Bassanio has found a usurer who can lend the money he needs. Shylock is very cautious, repeating each of Bassanio's demands to make sure that they are perfectly understood. His deliberation makes Bassanio nervous, and he shows irritation when Shylock says that 'Antonio is a good man'. The word 'good' has different implications: Bassanio thinks that it refers to Antonio's character, and he is angry that such a man as Shylock should presume to judge his friend. Shylock, having succeeded in annoying Bassanio, hastens to explain that by 'good' he meant only 'sufficient'—financially sound. The two disagree again over the interpretation of 'assur'd', by which Bassanio means that Shylock may trust Antonio; Shylock says that he will indeed be 'assur'd', meaning that he will take all precautions to protect himself and his money.

Bassanio's polite invitation to dinner is refused by Shylock in words that introduce the theme of racial hatred: he thinks he would be asked 'to smell pork', a meat forbidden to Jews by their religion. Shylock perhaps speaks these words '*aside*', not talking directly to Bassanio but uttering his thoughts aloud for the audience alone to hear them, just as only the audience hears the soliloquy in which Shylock reveals his attitude to Antonio. Religious feeling has some part in this attitude, but a minor one compared with the enmity he bears towards a business rival.

We learn that Antonio disapproves morally of lending money for interest (and it is a mark of his affection for Bassanio that he is prepared now to break his own rules). Shylock justifies his activities by telling the story of Jacob from the Old Testament (Genesis 30:31–43). Jacob was angry with Laban, his uncle, and tried to outwit him, using his skill as a shepherd. He believed that the ewes, seeing the striped twigs in front of them when they conceived, would give birth to striped or spotted lambs, which Laban had agreed should become Jacob's wages. This indeed happened, but whereas Shylock applauds Jacob's cunning, Antonio (and most devout Jews) ascribed the success to the hand of God.

The merchant and the usurer engage in passionate argument. Shylock reveals the cruel insults he has had to suffer from Antonio in the past, but Antonio stands firm in his contempt for the Jew. He refuses to borrow the money as a friend, but urges Shylock, with words that he will regret, to

> lend it rather to thine enemy,
> Who if he break, thou may'st with better face
> Exact the penalty.

Shylock proposes 'a merry sport' which Antonio, surprisingly, is willing to accept. He agrees to the forfeit that Shylock suggests—'an equal pound of your fair flesh'—to be given if the money cannot be properly repaid.

The words 'kind' and 'kindness' are repeated several times at the end of this scene. They have a surface meaning—'generous' and 'generosity'—which Antonio accepts, and an ironic double meaning. If Shylock 'grows kind' in this second sense, he will become even more like himself, true to his nature. And we have already, in his soliloquy, seen what this is.

Act 2

Scene 1 Prejudice is the subject of the short episode in Belmont, where we see Portia's reception of the Prince of Morocco. The prince's appearance shows that he is an exotic figure: the stage direction, probably written by Shakespeare himself, describes him as 'a tawny [brown] Moor, all in white'. His first speech reinforces our sense that he is excitingly different from the Europeans that we have seen so far, but it does not change Portia's mind. She is polite, but we understand, better than Morocco can, what she means when she tells him that, in her eyes, he is 'as fair As any comer I have look'd on yet'. We have heard what Portia thought of her other suitors. The Prince's reply to this ambiguous remark does not encourage our good opinion of him. He boasts of his own valour and achievements in a very exaggerated language, and so loses some of our sympathy.

We are given a new piece of information concerning the casket test. The men who choose wrongly must never again think of marrying. It is now clear why the earlier suitors left Belmont without trying their luck; Morocco, however, is not deterred, and prepares to make his choice.

Whilst Morocco is taking his oath in the 'temple'—many great houses at this time had their own private chapels—Shakespeare returns us to Venice. The next five scenes will bring Bassanio from Venice to Belmont, and develop the romance of the plot through the introduction of Jessica, Shylock's daughter. But first, Shakespeare must create a role for the leading comic actor in his dramatic company—the part of Lancelot Gobbo, Shylock's servant.

Scene 2 Comedy scenes such as this are the most difficult and unrewarding to read; they need to be performed, so that the actor can introduce the visual effects that the lines demand. When Lancelot pretends to be torn between his conscience and the devil, he might (for instance) jump to the left when the devil is speaking—because devils traditionally appeared on the left—and to the right when 'conscience' replies. There could be humour in the difference between Lancelot's appearance (as the miserly Shylock's servant he would not be well dressed) and his grand manner of speech to the old man; this would emphasize the comedy of the 'mistaken identity' situation. When Old Gobbo feels his son's head and comments on his 'beard', it is obvious from Lancelot's reply that he has got hold of the hair tied at the back of his neck; and if Lancelot passes his father's hand across his fingers, implying that they are his ribs ('You may tell every finger I have with my ribs'), the comedy will increase with the old man's bewilderment.

The English language is a very complicated one, and even English people make mistakes when they speak it. There are many words that sound grand—but sometimes those who use them do not understand their meanings, or else confuse one word with another that sounds similar. This is especially likely to happen when the speakers are trying to create a good impression of themselves. Lancelot and his father are doing this when they address Bassanio. They are conscious that Bassanio is a gentleman, whilst they are only peasants, and they try to use what they think is the proper language of gentlemen. Even in the twenty-first century, when class distinctions are much less clearly marked than they were in the sixteenth, the writers of television comedy still find subjects for laughter in our linguistic snobbishness. Lorenzo's comment is valid today: 'How every fool can play upon the word' (3, 5, 38).

Bassanio is in a good temper, and responds well to Lancelot's fooling; he agrees to employ him and give him 'a livery More guarded than his fellows'. A 'guarded' uniform—one decorated with yellow braid—was often worn by the professional fool in a gentleman's household; perhaps this is the function that Bassanio intends for Lancelot when he becomes 'The follower of so poor a gentleman'.

Even though he admits he is poor, Bassanio is already behaving with his former extravagance now that he has got Shylock's money. He is planning to give a party before he leaves Venice. However, he shows a more sedate side of his character when Gratiano asks to accompany him to Belmont. Gratiano turns Bassanio's solemn warning into comedy. He promises to behave in a way that is very sober, but at the same time quite ridiculous, and he probably accompanies his speech with exaggerated gestures.

Scene 3 When Jessica gives Lancelot the letter for Lorenzo, the short scene takes the plot a stride further—and also serves to increase our dislike for Shylock. We learn that his 'house is hell', and that Jessica is 'asham'd to be [her] father's child', although she recognizes that it is a 'heinous sin' for a daughter to have such feelings.

Scene 4 The letter is delivered to Lorenzo when he and his friends are discussing their costumes for Bassanio's party. It was quite usual, in Shakespeare's time, for a small band of the guests at a grand feast to disguise themselves in elaborate costumes and entertain the other guests with a masque—a performance with singing and dancing. Page-boys carried torches for the masquers, and Lorenzo suddenly realizes how he can steal Jessica away from her father's house: she can be disguised as his page.

Scene 5 There can scarcely be a greater contrast than that between the lively young men planning their evening's entertainment, and the surly Shylock. He takes no pleasure in the feast, but has decided to 'go in hate, to feed upon The prodigal Christian' (yet another comparison of Bassanio with the Prodigal Son). Shylock is determined to do all he can to ruin Bassanio, and he even considers that Lancelot's change of employer might 'help to waste His borrow'd purse'.

Scene 6 Gratiano's reference to the 'penthouse' under which they are standing is one of many remarks in Elizabethan drama that help us to reconstruct, in imagination, the kind of stage that Shakespeare was writing for. It seems that there was always a balcony, which allowed 'split-level' acting. In this scene the young men assemble on the main stage, underneath the 'penthouse' formed by the balcony on which Jessica appears, dressed as a boy. She is shy, because in Elizabethan times women *never* wore men's clothes. Her embarrassment is expressed with great delicacy, and it is easy to forget that Shakespeare and his contemporaries would probably have been a little amused by the situation. In many plays of this period the female characters put on masculine clothing, and a gentle comedy arises out of the fact that female characters were always played by boy actors: the boys dress up as girls, and then the 'girls' turn into boys.

Waiting for Jessica has made the masquers late for the feast, and now Antonio comes in search of Gratiano. The wind has changed, and it is time to set sail for Belmont.

Scene 7 Whilst all the activity of Jessica's elopement was taking place in Venice, the Prince of Morocco at Belmont has dined, and sworn an oath never to look for a wife if he fails the casket test. At last we see the caskets that we have heard so much about. Each one bears an inscription, which

Morocco reads aloud. The gold and silver caskets make promises, but the leaden one is menacing. Morocco refuses to be threatened, and passes to the silver casket, which assures him that he 'shall get as much as he deserves'. We heard in *Act 2*, Scene 1 that he has a good opinion of himself, and he is naturally tempted to choose silver. The golden casket, however, offers 'what many men desire', and Morocco decides that this refers to Portia, because 'all the world desires her'. It would be an insult to Portia (he concludes) to associate her with lead, or even with silver; so he opens the golden casket.

The casket contains a skull, the emblem of death—which indeed many unhappy men do desire. Shocked and saddened, the Prince of Morocco departs immediately.

Scene 8 In Venice, Shylock has discovered that his daughter is missing—and she has taken a lot of his money with her. Solanio gives a comical account of the Jew's confusion, when Shylock apparently did not know which loss to lament more. It is important that we do not *see* Shylock here, because his distress might create too much sympathy for him. Instead, we join Salarino and Solanio in their laughter.

But not everything in this scene is comic: there is bad news for Antonio. A ship has been wrecked in the English Channel, and it may well be his. The conversation becomes sober, as the two friends think of Antonio's generosity—'A kinder gentleman treads not the earth'—and remind us of his great affection for Bassanio: 'I think he only loves the world for him'.

Scene 9 Yet another suitor, the Prince of Arragon, has arrived at Belmont; he repeats the three promises that he has sworn to keep, and goes to make his choice of the three caskets. Like the Prince of Morocco, he reads the inscriptions, and speaks his thoughts aloud. The Prince of Arragon is excessively conscious of his social position, and insists that he is different from other men: he will not 'jump with common spirits', and look in the golden casket for 'what many men desire'. He is attracted by the promise of the silver casket: 'Who chooseth me shall get as much as he deserves'. For a time he meditates on the subject of nobility and merit, deploring the fact that 'low peasantry' (people of humble birth) can be found among noblemen—'the true seed of honour'. Having convinced *himself* that he deserves to win Portia, he opens the silver casket. We are not surprised that this is the wrong choice, for Arragon has convinced *us* that he is far too conceited—although perhaps he deserves something better than 'the portrait of a blinking idiot'.

As soon as the Prince of Arragon has left, news is brought that another suitor is approaching. He has already made a good impression on Portia's servants with the 'Gifts of rich value' that he has sent to announce his coming; and we recognize the extravagance that is characteristic of Bassanio. Portia and Nerissa are hopeful.

Act 3

Scene 1 The optimism of Belmont gives place to the darkening atmosphere of Venice. There is still no confirmation that the ship wrecked in the English Channel is indeed Antonio's, but Solanio believes the rumour to be true. Shylock also has heard the report, and his anger over his daughter's flight is forgotten for a moment as he gives expression to his hatred and resentment of Antonio. He has had to suppress his feelings for years, but now they explode violently. His passion increases, and so too does the sympathy of the audience. He appeals to common humanity: 'Hath not a Jew eyes? hath not a Jew hands . . . if you poison us, do we not die?' He becomes almost a hero, and certainly a human being—then suddenly he changes back into a monster: 'and if you wrong us, shall we not revenge?'

Salarino and Solanio are fortunately saved from having to reply to this tirade; they leave Shylock with another Jew, Tubal, who has news of Jessica.

Shylock experiences another confusion of emotions as Tubal imparts various pieces of information in an incoherent manner. Jessica is spending her father's money recklessly, and in exchange for a pet monkey she has given away the ring that was a token of betrothal from her mother to her father. Grief and anger conflict with malicious glee when Shylock hears of Antonio's misfortunes, and it is clear that he will take revenge for the loss of his daughter and his ring when he claims the forfeit from Antonio.

Scene 2 Portia is happy in Bassanio's company, and she tries to persuade him to stay at Belmont for a few days before making his choice of the caskets. Her happiness is mingled with modesty, for she is too shy to tell Bassanio that she loves him. Bassanio too has fallen in love, but he cannot endure the uncertainty and feels that he must try his luck as soon as possible. Nerissa and the servants stand aside, leaving Portia and Bassanio almost alone on the stage. Music plays, while Portia watches the man she loves as he tries to make the decision that will bring happiness to both of them.

The song that helps to create a magic atmosphere also introduces Bassanio's meditation on appearance and reality. He is speaking only to himself—Portia does not hear him (just as he did not hear her words before the song). The audience, of course, knows which casket Bassanio must choose, because Shakespeare has already shown us the contents of the gold and silver caskets.

Portia is almost overcome with delight when Bassanio selects the 'meagre lead'; and when Bassanio finds 'Fair Portia's counterfeit' in the casket he is ecstatically happy. He praises the picture rapturously, and for a time cannot believe his luck.

A rather more materialistic note is heard in the metaphorical language when Portia wishes to 'stand high in [Bassanio's] *account*', and offers him 'the full *sum*' of herself; it is repeated when Gratiano refers to the '*bargain*' of their faith. But to balance this there is the ritual moment when Portia gives away all that she owns (including 'this same myself') and as a token places a ring on Bassanio's finger. Bassanio accepts the token, and binds himself to Portia:

when this ring
Parts from this finger, then parts life from hence.

Gratiano and Nerissa announce their intention of imitating Bassanio and Portia; and the happiness of the moment is complete.

It is now time to change the direction of the scene, and Shakespeare switches the mood with a bawdy joke (in prose).

The arrival of Salerio, Lorenzo, and Jessica is a welcome surprise, but the letter that Salerio has brought from Venice 'steals the colour from Bassanio's cheek'. Things have gone very badly for Antonio: he is ruined. Salerio can tell of Shylock's eagerness to claim his bond from Antonio, and Jessica is able to bear witness to her father's fiendish malice: 'he would rather have Antonio's flesh Than twenty times the value of the sum That he did owe him'. Portia is more than able to pay back the three thousand ducats, but we can take no comfort from her offer. The situation seems hopeless, and when Antonio's pathetic letter is read aloud it destroys the last remaining scrap of the happiness established in the scene.

Scene 3 A short scene shows us what the letter described. Antonio, in the custody of a jailer, meets Shylock. The Jew will hear no pleas for mercy, and Antonio knows that it is useless to speak to him. Solanio hopes that the Duke will be able to intervene in the dispute, but Antonio knows the importance of strict justice in the mercantile world of which Venice is the head. This is a subject that will be mentioned at Antonio's trial.

Scene 4 Lorenzo has been telling Portia about Antonio, and Portia has decided that she and Nerissa will go away for a few days, leaving Belmont in the care of Lorenzo. She sends a servant to her cousin in Padua, asking for some 'notes and garments'. We understand the request for clothes when Portia explains to Nerissa that they are going to dress up as men, and that she herself will imitate all the mannerisms of a brash young man—including the voice that is 'between the change of man and boy'.

Scene 5 The next scene, still at Belmont, does nothing to develop any plot. But it encourages the audience to imagine that enough time has passed to allow Portia and Nerissa to travel from Belmont to Venice; on a practical level, it gives the actors time to change from their female dresses to the male costumes required in the following scene. In addition, it provides an opportunity for the comedian to deliver some more of his word-play jokes in the part of Lancelot Gobbo—who of course accompanied his new master when Bassanio came to Belmont.

Act 4

Scene 1 The trial scene in *The Merchant of Venice* is the most famous scene in English drama. It has given a phrase to the English language: people who have never read the play—and perhaps never even heard of it—understand what it means to want one's 'pound of flesh'.

The conversation between the Duke and Antonio, before Shylock comes on to the stage, shows the hopeless resignation with which Antonio faces Shylock's wrath. The Duke makes a further plea for mercy, but Shylock is unmoved. He will admit that his hatred for Antonio is irrational and emotional: just as some people hate cats, or the sound of bagpipes, so (he says)

> can I give no reason, nor I will not,
> More than a lodg'd hate and a certain loathing
> I bear Antonio.

Antonio is not intimidated, and shows his contempt for Shylock's 'Jewish heart'. Bassanio offers to repay twice the money that he borrowed, but Shylock will not yield, and reminds the court that the pound of flesh is his by law. If the Duke refuses to grant this, it will appear that 'There is no force in the decrees of Venice'. We remember Antonio's words (3, 3, 26–31), and realize that, if the law is not observed, Venice will suffer in its reputation as the centre of international trade.

The Duke has made a final attempt to save Antonio legally. He has asked for the opinion of a famous lawyer, Bellario, and the court waits to hear this man's judgement. Bassanio is optimistic, but the tension of the situation has made Antonio even more resigned to his fate; he almost feels that he deserves to die.

The lawyer's clerk has brought a letter from Bellario, and whilst the Duke reads the letter, Shylock sharpens his knife. Gratiano cannot bear to see this sight, and he begins to abuse Shylock. The Jew appears to be unaffected by his insults, for he knows the strength of his position: 'I stand here for law'.

Bellario is sick, and cannot come to Venice; instead he has sent a legal colleague, 'a young doctor of Rome', who is fully acquainted with the case. The audience recognizes this 'doctor': it is Portia, and her 'clerk' is Nerissa—but, needless to say, the other characters of the play cannot penetrate the disguise.

Portia upholds Venetian law, but she urges Shylock to show mercy. She describes the 'quality of mercy' as a divine blessing, which benefits both the man who shows mercy and the man who receives it. The petition in the Lord's Prayer, 'forgive us our trespasses', comes to mind when Portia explains how mercy belongs to God; if this were not so, the whole human race would be damned for its sins. But this is Christian doctrine, and Shylock's religion is that of the Old Testament, which emphasizes the importance of the law, just as Shylock does now: 'I crave the law'.

Once again Bassanio offers the money; again Shylock refuses it; and once more we are reminded that a general principle lies beneath this particular instance: any deviation would be

> recorded for a precedent,
> And many an error by the same example
> Will rush into the state.

The statement is harsh, but it is correct. Portia has earned Shylock's praise 'A Daniel come to judgement'. Daniel was 'a young youth', according to the 'Story of Susannah' in the *Apocrypha*. He was inspired by God to give judgement when the chaste Susannah was accused of adultery by two lascivious 'elders' who had tried to rape her.

Portia continues to win Shylock's approval as she instructs the court about the penalty that Antonio must pay. The knife is sharpened, and the scales are ready; Antonio prepares for death. He speaks a few words of comfort to Bassanio, ending with a wry jest about the debt:

> For if the Jew do cut but deep enough
> I'll pay it instantly with all my heart.

The tension is broken, but only for a moment, when Bassanio and Gratiano refer to their wives. The 'lawyer' and his 'clerk' are amused.

Just when Shylock is ready to cut into Antonio's flesh, Portia stops the proceedings. She reveals to Shylock the single flaw in his carefully worded bond: he is entitled to his pound of flesh, but has made no provision for a single drop of blood.

Gratiano exults over Shylock, repeating ironically all the words of praise that the Jew bestowed on the 'learned judge', and agreeing that he is indeed 'A second Daniel'. Like Portia, Daniel was not expected in the court, and the verdict he gave saved Susannah and condemned her accusers. The comparison is more apt now than it was when Shylock introduced it.

Shylock realizes that he cannot have his pound of flesh, and he tries to take the money that Bassanio is still offering. Now it is Portia's turn to be inflexible, and she insists that Shylock can have 'merely justice, and his bond'. When Shylock proposes to leave the court, Portia calls him back. The law of Venice has a strict penalty that must be paid by any 'alien'—foreigner—who tries to murder a Venetian. Shylock has thus offended, and for this crime his possessions are confiscated and his life is in danger. Antonio, of course, shows his generosity. Half of Shylock's wealth is forfeited to him, but he is willing to renounce his personal share and take the money on loan, keeping it in trust for Lorenzo, 'the gentleman That lately stole his daughter'. He makes two conditions: firstly, Shylock must become a Christian; and, secondly, he must make a will leaving all that he possesses to Jessica and Lorenzo. Shylock is utterly defeated. He asks for permission to leave the court, and indicates his agreement to Antonio's conditions: 'send the deed after me And I will sign it'.

It is now the function of Gratiano to swing the mood of the scene and the audience from near-tragedy to an almost light-hearted acceptance of the situation: this is only a play, and we are in England, where twelve 'godfathers' would make a jury.

It is only necessary now to pay the 'lawyer', and then Bassanio can take Antonio home to Belmont, to meet his new wife. The 'lawyer' refuses payment, then suddenly catches sight of a ring on Bassanio's finger, and requests this as a keepsake. It is the ring that Portia gave to Bassanio, telling him that if he should ever part with it for any reason, it would 'presage the ruin of [his] love'. Remembering this, Bassanio refuses; the 'lawyer' departs, apparently angry. Antonio begs Bassanio not to withhold the ring, and Bassanio cannot refuse the friend who risked so much for him.

Scene 2 Gratiano hurries after Portia to give her Bassanio's ring. Nerissa, still disguised as the lawyer's clerk, whispers to Portia that she will use a similar trick to get her own ring from Gratiano. The two girls laugh in anticipation of their husbands' embarrassment when they return to Belmont.

Act 5

Scene 1 Moonlight and music emphasize the tranquillity of Belmont and its contrast with the harsh legal world of Venice. Lorenzo and Jessica are relaxed here, and Jessica's escape from the 'hell' of her father's house seems to be almost as remote in time as the mythological lovers who are recalled by the moonlight. The mood of the scene is saved from being over-romantic when the couple start to tease each other, and when the messengers break in with their news. Harmony is restored, however, when Lorenzo and Jessica are alone again. Lorenzo starts to explain the theory of the music of the spheres, made by the planets in their constant motion but beyond the hearing of human ears, which are deafened by the noises of earthly life.

Portia's musicians appear, probably on the balcony, to 'draw [their mistress] home with music'. The beauty of Lorenzo's speech (when he describes the 'patens of bright gold', and the 'young-eyed cherubins') blends with the playing of the musicians to re-create, in human terms, the heavenly harmony. Lorenzo and Jessica fall silent; perhaps they are asleep.

Portia and Nerissa come from the opposite side of the stage as they approach Belmont from Venice. Their chatter breaks into the music, and the dream world becomes real. A trumpet announces the arrival of Bassanio, just as day is breaking. The missing rings provide a final gentle comedy, as the two embarrassed husbands try to justify their actions to wives who are trying to hide their amusement.

In the end, of course, all is happiness. Lorenzo and Jessica join the other two couples, and Portia gives Antonio a last surprise—the news that three of his ships 'Are richly come to harbour suddenly'. There can be no reaction from the audience other than Antonio's 'I am dumb', and final applause for Shakespeare. He has taken three main strands—the casket story, the bond story, and the ring story—and woven them into a single plot, which brings all three stories to a successful conclusion, and ensures that all the characters (with one exception) 'live happily ever after'—just as fairy-tale characters ought to do.

Shylock

A happy ending for the leading characters is essential for a romantic comedy such as *The Merchant of Venice*. But one very important character is left out of the general rejoicing in Act 5. Shylock has been defeated of his bond, robbed of his ducats, and deserted by his daughter; he is even compelled to give up his birthright, his Jewish religion, and become one of the Christians whom he so much hates. Does he deserve this fate? Is *The Merchant of Venice* a comedy for all the other characters, but a tragedy for Shylock?

Shakespeare took the story of Shylock's bond from an Italian novel, but the money-lending Jew in this source has no personality, and no daughter. Consequently we can assume that Shylock is Shakespeare's own creation: all the personality traits that we find in him were deliberately worked out by the dramatist, and not borrowed accidentally along with the plot.

Shylock starts from a double disadvantage, as far as an Elizabethan audience was concerned. He is a Jew, and he is a money-lender. There were not many Jews in England, but in the Middle Ages English Christians hated the Jews, and this feeling was still strong in the sixteenth century. The Elizabethans also hated the traditional Jewish profession of usury—the lending of money for profit. Jews were often forbidden to own land or to engage in trade in England; consequently the only lucrative profession open to them was money-lending. The Christians deplored this—in theory. In practice, the expanding economy of the times demanded that money should be readily available. Francis Bacon, who was Lord Chancellor of England in 1618, claimed that

> to speak of the abolishing of usury is idle. All states have ever had it, in one kind, or rate, or other. So as that opinion must be sent to Utopia. (Essay 'Of Usury')

Certainly, the usurer is necessary to the world of *The Merchant of Venice*. Shylock's wealth is evidence of his professional success, which could only come from satisfying a social need.

Shylock first appears as the cautious businessman, thinking carefully before he invests his three thousand ducats in Bassanio's enterprise. His reaction to the polite invitation to dinner is unexpected in its venom, which increases as he tells the audience of his hatred for Antonio.

Religious differences seem to be less important than professional jealousy:

> I hate him for he is a Christian;
> But more for that in low simplicity
> He lends out money gratis.

To some extent Shylock justifies his hostility when he describes how he has been treated by Antonio—insulted, spat upon, and kicked out of the way like 'a stranger cur'. Because of this, we sympathize with him. When the scene ends, we are left with two conflicting opinions of Shylock and his 'merry sport'. Are we to share Antonio's surprise, 'And say there is much kindness in the Jew'? Or is Bassanio right to be suspicious of 'fair terms and a villain's mind'?

The scene with Antonio and Bassanio shows Shylock in his professional, public, life. Next, we hear what he is like at home. His comic servant, Lancelot Gobbo, exaggerates (with a characteristic misuse of the English language) when he says that 'the Jew is the very devil incarnation'. But this opinion is echoed by Shylock's daughter, Jessica, when she sighs 'Our house is hell'. Jessica is 'asham'd to be [her] father's child', although she knows that it is a 'heinous sin' for a daughter to have such feelings. We can understand Jessica's misery when her father gives instructions about locking up his house whilst he is away. Jessica is forbidden even to look out of the window to watch the masquers going to Bassanio's feast. Shylock is a kill-joy—and he has also killed his daughter's natural affection for him.

Shakespeare does not let us see Shylock in his first frenzy of distress when he finds that Jessica is missing, because this would surely arouse our sympathy. Instead, Solanio describes the scene, and the audience is encouraged to share in his laughter. From Solanio's account, it seems that Shylock's grief over the loss of his daughter is equalled (perhaps even surpassed) by his anger at the theft of his money. He utters 'a passion so confus'd':

> My daughter! O my ducats! O my daughter!
> Fled with a Christian! O my Christian ducats!

When Shylock next appears (*Act 3*, Scene 1) the passion is subdued into an intense and malevolent bitterness; yet the jesting of the two Christians is cruel. The loss of a daughter is a real cause for sorrow, and Shylock earns some pity (from the audience) when he tells Solanio and Salarino that 'my daughter is my flesh and my blood'.

It is with very mixed feelings, then, that we are led up to the powerful speech in which Shylock catalogues the abuses he has had to suffer from Christians in general, and from Antonio in particular. There is only one reason that he can see for this treatment: 'I am a Jew'. It is easy to respond to the rhetorical questions that follow:

> Hath not a Jew eyes? hath not a Jew hands, organs, dimensions, senses, affections, passions? fed with the same food, hurt with the same weapons, subject to the same diseases, healed by the same means, warmed and cooled by the same winter and summer, as a Christian is? if you prick us, do we not bleed? if you tickle us, do we not laugh? if you poison us, do we not die?

Shylock appeals to our common humanity. To give a negative answer to his questions would deny not *his* humanity, but our own. The speech, however, continues:

> and if you wrong us, shall we not revenge? If we are like you in the rest, we will resemble you in that . . . The villainy you teach me I will execute, and it shall go hard but I will better the instruction.

Common humanity ignores all limitations of colour, race, or creed; and this is strongly asserted in the first part of Shylock's speech. But the assertions of these last lines show that the individual—Shylock—is determined to ignore the limits of humanity. He will 'better the instruction', and prove himself to be not the *equal* of the Christians in inflicting suffering on others, but their *superior*.

The events that follow do nothing to moderate the presentation of Shylock in the terms used by the Duke when he warns Antonio, before the trial begins, that his adversary is

> an inhuman wretch
> Uncapable of pity, void and empty
> From any dram of mercy.

During the trial, Shylock loses the audience's sympathy, by his words and by the action of sharpening the knife on the sole of his shoe (which Gratiano observes in line 123). Neither insults nor pleading spoil the enjoyment of his triumph, and when sentence is given against Antonio, he repeats the words of the bond with a lingering relish:

> Ay, 'his breast':
> So says the bond—doth it not, noble judge?—
> 'Nearest his heart'—those are the very words.

Shylock demanded a strict observance of the law, and (in poetic justice) it is precisely this that defeats him. Gratiano exults over his downfall, but the other characters in the court speak no unnecessary words and show no satisfaction until Shylock has left the court. Even then, conversation is formal, occupied only with thanks and payment. It does not obliterate the memory of Shylock's parting words:

> I pray you give me leave to go from hence:
> I am not well.

A snarl of frustrated wrath can deliver this line; or else it can be spoken with the anguish of a man who has lost everything—his daughter, his wealth, his religious freedom, and the engagement ring given to him by his wife.

Recent English productions of *The Merchant of Venice* have emphasized the suffering human being, but I do not think that this is what Shakespeare intended. Shylock is more complex than any of the other characters in the play: we can think of him as a 'real' person, whose words and deeds are motivated by thoughts and feelings that we can discover from the play, and that we can understand when we have discovered them. We cannot think of Bassanio (for instance) in this way. Yet in admiring Shakespeare's achievement in the creation of Shylock, we must beware of danger. Often, when we know a person well, and understand why he acts as he does, we become sympathetic to him; in *The Merchant of Venice* we are further encouraged to sympathize with Shylock also by the fact that other leading characters (such as Bassanio) do *not* compel our sympathies. Sympathy can give rise to affection, and affection often tempts us to withhold moral judgement, or at least be gentle in our censure. Shylock's conduct merits condemnation. We can only refrain from condemning it because we know that he has suffered for being a Jew; and this, surely, is another form of prejudice?

Shakespeare's Verse

Easily the best way to understand and appreciate Shakespeare's verse is to read it aloud—and don't worry if you can't understand everything! Try not to be captivated by the dominant rhythm, but decide which are the most important words in each line and use the regular metre to drive them forward to the listeners.

Shakespeare's plays are mainly written in 'blank verse', the form preferred by most dramatists in the sixteenth and early seventeenth centuries. It is a very flexible medium, which is capable—like the human speaking voice—of a wide range of tones. Basically, the lines, which are unrhymed, are ten syllables long. The syllables have alternating stresses, just like normal English speech; and they divide into five 'feet'. The technical name for this is 'iambic pentameter'.

Solanio
Beliéve me, sír, had Í such vénture fórth,
The bétter párt of mý affections woúld
Be wíth my hópes abróad. I shoúld be stíll
Plúcking the gráss to knów where síts the wínd,
Píring in máps for pórts, and piérs, and róads;
And évery óbject thát might máke me feár
Misfórtune tó my véntures, oút of doúbt
Would máke me sád.
Salarino
My wínd coolíng my bróth
Would blów me tó an águe whén I thoúght
What hárm a wínd too gréat might dó at seá. *1, 1, 15–24*

Here the pentameter accommodates a variety of speech tones—Solanio starts with the simple, conversational expression 'Believe me'; then his speech becomes more dramatic as his imagination takes hold of the subject. Salarino, speaking on the same theme, joins in halfway through a line, as though he were singing the same tune as Solanio.

In this quotation, the lines are fairly regular in length and mostly normal in iambic stress pattern. Solanio's 'every' must be given only two syllables ('ev'ry') as in much modern English speech; and the stresses on 'Plucking' and 'Piring' are not iambic—an irregularity which adds dramatic emphasis.

Sometimes the verse line contains the grammatical unit of meaning—'Piring in maps for ports, and piers, and roads'—thus allowing for a pause at the end of the line, before a new idea is started; at other times, the sense runs on from one line to the next—'I should be still Plucking the grass to know where sits the wind'. This makes for natural fluidity of speech, avoiding monotony but still maintaining the iambic rhythm.

Source, Date, and Text

Popular fiction (see 'Sources', p.101) provided the plot outlines, and a rival dramatist's play gave inspiration for the character of Shylock in *The Merchant of Venice,* and the play must have been written at some time after June 1596, when an English expedition made a surprise attack on four richly appointed Spanish galleons in Cadiz harbour. In the fighting these cut adrift and ran aground, and two of them, the *San Matias* and the *San Andrès,* were captured and brought in triumph back to England. It is, almost certainly, this event that Salarino is referring to in *Act 1*, Scene 1, lines 25–9:

> I should not see the sandy hourglass run
> But I should think of shallows and of flats,
> And see my wealthy Andrew dock'd in sand,
> Vailing her high top lower than her ribs
> To kiss her burial.

The merit of Shakespeare's comedy was already recognized by 1598, when it was praised by Francis Meres in his account of the best contemporary English writing, *Palladis Tamia* (registered for publication September 1598).

The earliest text of the play, published in 1600, was probably based on Shakespeare's own manuscript, and reproduces the author's own detailed (but often imprecise) stage directions. The present edition is based on the text established by M. M. Mahood for the Cambridge Shakespeare in 1987.

Characters in the Play

The Duke of Venice	
The Prince of Morocco **The Prince of Arragon**	*suitors to* Portia
Bassanio	*an Italian lord, suitor to* Portia
Antonio	*a merchant of Venice, friend of* Bassanio
Solanio **Salarino** **Gratiano** **Lorenzo**	*gentlemen of Venice, friends of* Bassanio
Shylock	*the rich Jew, a money-lender*
Jessica	*his daughter*
Tubal	*another Jew,* Shylock*'s friend*
Lancelot Gobbo	*servant to* Shylock
Old Gobbo	Lancelot*'s father*
Portia	*a rich Italian lady*
Nerissa	*her lady-in-waiting*
Stephano	*a messenger*
Leonardo	Bassanio*'s servant*
Salerio	*a messenger from Venice*
Balthazar	Portia*'s servant*
Jailer	
	Other servingmen, messengers, merchants, officers, court officials, musicians

'Rest you fair, good signor! Your worship was the last man in our mouths' (*1*, 3, 54–5).
Henry Goodman as Shylock, Royal National Theatre, 1999.

ACT 1

Act 1 Scene 1
Antonio is depressed; his friends cannot cheer him, but he is only too willing to lend his money to Bassanio.

0s.d. *Salarino*: Some editors print 'Salerio' here, doubling Antonio's business colleague with Portia's messenger.
1 *In sooth*: truly.
2 *It*: his sadness.
3 *came by*: got.
5 *am to learn*: do not know.
6 *want-wit*: idiot.
7 *ado*: trouble.
9 *argosies*: merchant ships.
portly: stately.
10 *signors*: gentleman (the modern Italian word is *signori*).
burghers: citizens.
flood: sea.
11 *pageants*: decorated carts in carnival processions.
12 *overpeer*: look over the heads of.
petty traffickers: small commercial boats.
13 *That . . . reverence*: that bob up and down, as if they were showing respect.

15 *had . . . forth*: if I had such business abroad.
16 *affections*: concerns.
17 *still*: always.
18 *Plucking . . . wind*: holding up a blade of grass to see in which direction the wind is blowing.
19 *Piring in*: looking closely at, poring over.
roads: anchorages.
21 *out of doubt*: without doubt.

22 *wind*: breath.
broth: soup.
23 *ague*: fit of shivering.
25 *sandy hour-glass*: the sands in the hour-glass.
26 *shallows*: shallow waters.
flats: sandbanks.

SCENE 1

Venice: a street. Enter Antonio, Salarino, *and* Solanio

Antonio
In sooth I know not why I am so sad.
It wearies me, you say it wearies you;
But how I caught it, found it, or came by it,
What stuff 'tis made of, whereof it is born,
I am to learn.
And such a want-wit sadness makes of me,
That I have much ado to know myself.

Salarino
Your mind is tossing on the ocean,
There where your argosies with portly sail
Like signors and rich burghers on the flood,
Or as it were the pageants of the sea,
Do overpeer the petty traffickers
That curtsy to them, do them reverence,
As they fly by them with their woven wings.

Solanio
Believe me, sir, had I such venture forth,
The better part of my affections would
Be with my hopes abroad. I should be still
Plucking the grass to know where sits the wind,
Piring in maps for ports, and piers, and roads;
And every object that might make me fear
Misfortune to my ventures, out of doubt
Would make me sad.

Salarino
My wind cooling my broth
Would blow me to an ague when I thought
What harm a wind too great might do at sea.
I should not see the sandy hourglass run
But I should think of shallows and of flats,

And see my wealthy Andrew dock'd in sand,
Vailing her high top lower than her ribs
To kiss her burial. Should I go to church
And see the holy edifice of stone
And not bethink me straight of dangerous rocks,
Which touching but my gentle vessel's side
Would scatter all her spices on the stream,
Enrobe the roaring waters with my silks,
And (in a word) but even now worth this,
And now worth nothing? Shall I have the thought
To think on this, and shall I lack the thought
That such a thing bechanc'd would make me sad?
But tell not me: I know Antonio
Is sad to think upon his merchandise.

Antonio

Believe me, no. I thank my fortune for it,
My ventures are not in one bottom trusted,
Nor to one place; nor is my whole estate
Upon the fortune of this present year:
Therefore my merchandise makes me not sad.

Solanio

Why then, you are in love.

Antonio

Fie, fie!

27 *my wealthy Andrew*: my own richly-laden vessel; see 'Source, Date, and Text', p. xxxii.

28 *vailing her high top*: lowering her mast.
ribs: the wooden sides of the ship.

29 *burial*: burial-ground.

31 *straight*: immediately.

32 *touching but*: only by touching.
gentle: a) delicate; b) noble.

33–4 *spices . . . silks*: The luxury goods of Venetian trade.

34 *Enrobe*: clothe.

35 *in a word*: briefly.

35–6 *but . . . nothing*: highly valuable just a moment ago, then worth nothing.

36 *thought*: imagination.

38 *such . . . bechanc'd*: such a (disastrous) thing happening.

41 *fortune*: a) wealth; b) luck.

42 *ventures*: business.
bottom: ship.

44 *fortune*: chance.

46 *Fie, fie*: nonsense; two syllables are missing from this line—perhaps allowing for an embarrassed pause.

50 *Janus*: the two-heading Roman god of doorways and openings, who faced both directions at once.

52 *evermore*: always.
peep . . . eyes: screw up their eyes.
53 *laugh like parrots*: squawk with laughter.
bagpiper: Bagpipes make a melancholy, droning music.

54 *other*: others.
vinegar aspect: sour looks; 'aspect' is stressed on the second syllable.
56 *Nestor*: an old and wise Greek general who fought in the war against Troy.
57 *kinsman*: In Shakespeare's main source, the merchant ('Ansaldo') was the godfather of the younger man ('Giannetto').
61 *prevented*: forestalled, anticipated.
62 *regard*: esteem.
63 *calls on*: needs.
64 *embrace th'occasion*: welcome the opportunity.
66 *laugh*: meet together for fun.
67 *strange*: distant, unfriendly.
68 *We'll . . . yours*: we'll be free when you are.
71 *have in mind*: think about.
72 *I will . . . you*: This half-line could allow Lorenzo some gesture of farewell.

Solanio
Not in love neither? Then let us say you are sad
Because you are not merry; and 'twere as easy
For you to laugh and leap, and say you are merry
Because you are not sad. Now by two-headed Janus,
Nature hath fram'd strange fellows in her time:
Some that will evermore peep through their eyes,
And laugh like parrots at a bagpiper;
And other of such vinegar aspect,
That they'll not show their teeth in way of smile
Though Nestor swear the jest be laughable.

Enter Bassanio, Lorenzo, *and* Gratiano

Here comes Bassanio, your most noble kinsman,
Gratiano, and Lorenzo. Fare ye well;
We leave you now with better company.

Salarino
I would have stay'd till I had made you merry,
If worthier friends had not prevented me.

Antonio
Your worth is very dear in my regard.
I take it your own business calls on you,
And you embrace th'occasion to depart.

Salarino
Good morrow, my good lords.

Bassanio
Good signors both, when shall we laugh? Say, when?
You grow exceeding strange; must it be so?

Salarino
We'll make our leisures to attend on yours.
[*Exeunt* Salarino *and* Solanio

Lorenzo
My Lord Bassanio, since you have found Antonio
We two will leave you, but at dinner time
I pray you have in mind where we must meet.

Bassanio
I will not fail you.

Gratiano
You look not well, Signor Antonio.

74 *respect upon*: regard for.

75 *They . . . care*: those who worry too much about the world lose the ability to enjoy it.

76 *you . . . chang'd*: you have changed a lot.

77 *hold*: think of.

78 *A stage . . . part*: This Elizabethan commonplace became the motto of Shakespeare's Globe Theatre (*Totus mundus agit histrionem*—all the world plays the actor).

79 *Let . . . Fool*: 'Gratiano' was the name of a comic doctor in the Italian *commedia dell' arte*.

82 *mortifying groans*: Sighing was supposed to shorten life.

84 *his . . . alabaster*: a monumental statue of his grandfather.

85 *Sleep . . . wakes*: be still and silent all day.
jaundice: yellow sickness, thought by the Elizabethans to be of psychological origin.

87 *it is . . . speaks*: I'm saying this because I love you.

88–9 *whose . . . pond*: whose impassive faces are like stagnant ponds filmed over with algae.

90–1 *do . . . opinion*: maintain an obstinate silence in order to get a reputation.

92 *conceit*: thought.

93 *Sir Oracle*: a noble oracle (speaking with divine authority).

94 *ope*: open.
let . . . bark: don't interrupt.

95–7 *know . . . nothing*: know some of these men who are thought to be clever only because they never say anything.

99 *call . . . fools*: 'whosoever shall say to his brother . . . Thou fool, shall be in danger of hell fire' St Matthew, 5:22.

101–2 *fish . . . opinion*: don't use your melancholy to catch yourself an easy and worthless reputation; 'gudgeon' was a particularly gullible fish.

104 *exhortation*: sermon.

108 *moe*: more.

You have too much respect upon the world:
They lose it that do buy it with much care.
Believe me, you are marvellously chang'd.

Antonio

I hold the world but as the world, Gratiano:
A stage where every man must play a part,
And mine a sad one.

Gratiano

Let me play the Fool.
With mirth and laughter let old wrinkles come,
And let my liver rather heat with wine
Than my heart cool with mortifying groans.
Why should a man whose blood is warm within
Sit like his grandsire cut in alabaster?
Sleep when he wakes? And creep into the jaundice
By being peevish? I tell thee what, Antonio—
I love thee, and it is my love that speaks—
There are a sort of men whose visages
Do cream and mantle like a standing pond,
And do a wilful stillness entertain,
With purpose to be dress'd in an opinion
Of wisdom, gravity, profound conceit,
As who should say, 'I am Sir Oracle,
And when I ope my lips, let no dog bark!'
O my Antonio, I do know of these
That therefore only are reputed wise
For saying nothing; when I am very sure
If they should speak, would almost damn those ears
Which, hearing them, would call their brothers fools.
I'll tell thee more of this another time.
But fish not with this melancholy bait
For this fool gudgeon, this opinion.
Come, good Lorenzo. Fare ye well awhile;
I'll end my exhortation after dinner.

Lorenzo

Well, we will leave you then till dinner time.
I must be one of these same dumb wise men,
For Gratiano never lets me speak.

Gratiano

Well, keep me company but two years moe,
Thou shalt not know the sound of thine own tongue.

Antonio
Farewell; I'll grow a talker for this gear.

Gratiano
Thanks, i'faith, for silence is only commendable
In a neat's tongue dried, and a maid not vendible.
[*Exeunt* Gratiano *and* Lorenzo

Antonio
It is that anything now.

Bassanio
Gratiano speaks an infinite deal of nothing, more than any man in all Venice. His reasons are as two grains of wheat hid in two bushels of chaff: you shall seek all day ere you find them, and when you have them they are not worth the search.

Antonio
Well, tell me now what lady is the same
To whom you swore a secret pilgrimage
That you today promis'd to tell me of.

Bassanio
'Tis not unknown to you, Antonio,
How much I have disabled mine estate
By something showing a more swelling port
Than my faint means would grant continuance.
Nor do I now make moan to be abridg'd
From such a noble rate, but my chief care
Is to come fairly off from the great debts
Wherein my time, something too prodigal,
Hath left me gag'd. To you, Antonio,
I owe the most in money and in love,
And from your love I have a warranty
To unburden all my plots and purposes
How to get clear of all the debts I owe.

Antonio
I pray you, good Bassanio, let me know it,
And if it stand as you yourself still do
Within the eye of honour, be assur'd
My purse, my person, my extremest means
Lie all unlock'd to your occasions.

Bassanio
In my schooldays, when I had lost one shaft,
I shot his fellow of the selfsame flight

110 *grow . . . gear*: become more talkative for this reason.
112 *a neat's . . . vendible*: an impotent old man and an unmarriageable woman.
neat's tongue: ox-tongue, preserved for eating.
vendible: marketable.
113 *It is . . . now*: peace at last.
115 *reasons*: ideas.
117 *ere*: before.
122–34 *'Tis . . . I owe*: Bassanio is rather inarticulate in his embarrassment.
123 *disabled*: damaged.
124–5 *By . . . continuance*: by flaunting a rather more extravagant lifestyle ('port') than my limited means would allow me to continue.
126 *make . . . abridg'd*: complain about being forced to cut back.
127 *noble rate*: grand style.
care: concern.
128 *come fairly off*: extricate myself honourably.
129 *my time . . . prodigal*: my past, when I was spending rather too lavishly; Bassanio seems to compare himself with the Prodigal Son who spent his inheritance on riotous living (St Luke, chapter 15).
130 *gag'd*: owing.
132 *from . . . warranty*: your love authorizes me.
133 *unburden*: disclose to you.
purposes: plans.
136–7 *if . . . honour*: if your plan looks honourable, as you yourself have always been.
139 *occasions*: needs.
140 *shaft*: arrow.
141 *his fellow . . . flight*: an identical arrow of the same weight ('flight').

The selfsame way, with more advised watch
To find the other forth; and by adventuring both
I oft found both. I urge this childhood proof
Because what follows is pure innocence.
I owe you much, and like a wilful youth
That which I owe is lost; but if you please
To shoot another arrow that self way
Which you did shoot the first, I do not doubt,
As I will watch the aim, or to find both
Or bring your latter hazard back again
And thankfully rest debtor for the first.

Antonio

You know me well, and herein spend but time
To wind about my love with circumstance;
And out of doubt you do me now more wrong
In making question of my uttermost
Than if you had made waste of all I have.
Then do but say to me what I should do
That in your knowledge may by me be done,
And I am prest unto it: therefore speak.

Bassanio

In Belmont is a lady richly left,
And she is fair, and—fairer than that word—
Of wondrous virtues. Sometimes from her eyes
I did receive fair speechless messages.
Her name is Portia, nothing undervalued
To Cato's daughter, Brutus' Portia.
Nor is the wide world ignorant of her worth;
For the four winds blow in from every coast
Renowned suitors, and her sunny locks
Hang on her temples like a golden fleece,
Which makes her seat of Belmont Colchos' strand,
And many Jasons come in quest of her.
O my Antonio, had I but the means
To hold a rival place with one of them,
I have a mind presages me such thrift
That I should questionless be fortunate.

Antonio

Thou know'st that all my fortunes are at sea;
Neither have I money nor commodity

142 *advised*: advisèd; careful.

143 *find . . . forth*: to find out where the other was.
adventuring: risking.

144 *urge . . . proof*: I'm offering you this childhood example.

145 *innocence*: ingenuity.

148 *self*: selfsame.

150 *aim*: direction.

150–1 *or . . . Or*: either . . . or.

151 *hazard*: risk, gamble.

152 *rest debtor*: remain in debt.

153 *spend but time*: only waste time.

154 *To . . . circumstance*: in going such a roundabout way to make use of my love.

156 *making . . . uttermost*: doubting that I will give you every assistance.

157 *made waste of*: destroyed.

160 *prest unto*: ready to do.

161 *richly left*: who has inherited a fortune.

162 *fairer . . . word*: even better than that: Bassanio sets wealth, beauty, and virtue in ascending order of desirability.

163 *Sometimes*: at one time, formerly.

164 *speechless*: unspoken.

165–6 *nothing . . . Portia*: no less worthy than the historical Portia, daughter of a distinguished Roman tribune and the wife of Brutus, who led the conspiracy against Julius Caesar.

169 *Renowned*: renownèd.
sunny locks: golden hair.

170 *golden fleece*: In Greek mythology, Jason led an expedition to Colchis in search of the golden ram's fleece.

171 *seat*: house.
strand: shore.

172 *quest*: search.

173–4 *had I . . . them*: if I could become a rival with these suitors.

175 *presages*: prophesies.
thrift: profitable success.

176 *questionless*: without doubt.

177 *fortunes*: wealth.

178 *commodity*: merchandise.

179 *a present sum*: some ready money.
180 *Try . . . do*: see what you can borrow on my credit in Venice.
181 *rack'd*: stretched.
182 *furnish . . . Belmont*: provide what you need to go to Belmont.
183 *presently*: immediately.
184–5 *I . . . sake*: I'm sure you will get it either on my credit or for the sake of my friendship.

To raise a present sum; therefore go forth,
Try what my credit can in Venice do,
That shall be rack'd even to the uttermost
To furnish thee to Belmont to fair Portia.
Go presently enquire, and so will I,
Where money is, and I no question make
To have it of my trust or for my sake. [*Exeunt*

Act 1 Scene 2
Portia is rich, but she has not yet found a man who can pass her father's test to be her husband.

0s.d. *waiting-woman*: lady-in-waiting—a companion and confidante.
1 *troth*: faith.
aweary: tired; Portia seems to be as melancholy as Antonio.
1–2 *my . . . world*: Portia invokes the routine Elizabethan comparison between the little human world (microcosm) and the physical universe (macrocosm).
4 *in . . . abundance*: as plentiful.
5 *aught*: anything.
surfeit: eat excessively.
6–7 *no mean . . . mean*: no small happiness to be set in the middle; Nerissa plays on two senses of 'mean'.
8 *superfluity*: excess.
9 *competency*: adequacy.
10 *sentences*: proverbs.
pronounced: delivered.
11 followed: obeyed.
12–20 *If . . . cripple*: Portia can provide 'sentences' of her own.
13 *had been*: would be.
14 *divine*: preacher.
17 *blood*: will, passion; Portia recognizes the conflict between head and heart.
18–20 *such . . . cripple*: crazy young love, like a hare, easily eludes the snares of well-meaning but unfeeling advice.
20–1 *reasoning . . . husband*: talking like this isn't the right way to find myself a husband.
22 *I would*: I like.

Scene 2

Belmont: Portia*'s house. Enter* Portia *with her waiting-woman* Nerissa

Portia
By my troth, Nerissa, my little body is aweary of this great world.

Nerissa
You would be, sweet madam, if your miseries were in the same abundance as your good fortunes are; and yet for aught I see, they are as sick that surfeit with too much as they that starve with nothing. It is no mean happiness, therefore, to be seated in the mean—superfluity comes sooner by white hairs, but competency lives longer.

Portia
Good sentences, and well pronounced.

Nerissa
They would be better if well followed.

Portia
If to do were as easy as to know what were good to do, chapels had been churches, and poor men's cottages princes' palaces. It is a good divine that follows his own instructions; I can easier teach twenty what were good to be done, than be one of the twenty to follow mine own teaching. The brain may devise laws for the blood, but a hot temper leaps o'er a cold decree—such a hare is madness the youth, to skip o'er the meshes of good counsel the cripple. But this reasoning is not in the fashion to choose me a husband. O me, the word 'choose'! I may neither choose who I would, nor refuse

'I may neither choose who I would, nor refuse who I dislike' (*1*, 1, 22–3) Jane Carr as Nerissa and Joanna McCallum as Portia, Chichester Festival Theatre, 1984.

who I dislike, so is the will of a living daughter curbed by the will of a dead father. Is it not hard, Nerissa, that I cannot choose one, nor refuse none?

Nerissa

Your father was ever virtuous; and holy men at their death have good inspirations. Therefore the lottery that he hath devised in these three chests of gold, silver, and lead, whereof who chooses his meaning chooses you, will no doubt never be chosen by any rightly but one who you shall rightly love. But what warmth is there in your affection towards any of these princely suitors that are already come?

Portia

I pray thee over-name them, and as thou namest them I will describe them—and according to my description, level at my affection.

Nerissa

First, there is the Neapolitan prince.

Portia

Ay, that's a colt indeed, for he doth nothing but talk of his horse; and he makes it a great appropriation to his own good parts that he can shoe him himself. I am much afeared my lady his mother played false with a smith.

Nerissa

Then is there the County Palatine.

Portia

He doth nothing but frown, as who should say, 'And you will not have me, choose.' He hears merry tales and smiles not; I fear he will prove the weeping philosopher when he grows old, being so full of unmannerly sadness in his youth. I had rather be married to a death's head with a bone in his mouth than to either of these. God defend me from these two!

Nerissa

How say you by the French lord, Monsieur Le Bon?

Portia

God made him, and therefore let him pass for a man. In truth I know it is a sin to be a mocker, but he!—why, he hath a horse better than the Neapolitan's, a better bad habit of frowning than the Count Palatine: he is every

23 *will*: a) wish; b) sexual desire; c) testament.
curbed: restrained.

26 *ever*: always.

28 *these*: Apparently the caskets are already on the stage.

29 *his meaning*: the one he intended.

30 *rightly*: a) correctly; b) truly.

34 *over-name*: run through their names.

36 *level*: guess.

37 *Neapolitan*: Portia's suitors are all national stereotypes.

38 *colt*: uncouth young man.

38–9 *nothing . . . horse*: The southern Italians were famous for their horsemanship.

39–40 *appropriation . . . parts*: addition to his accomplishments.

42 *smith*: blacksmith.

43 *County Palatine*: i.e. a nobleman with royal privileges, holding jurisdiction over a province within an empire.

44 *as . . . say*: as if to say.
And: if.

45 *choose*: have it your own way.

46 *prove*: turn out like.
the weeping philosopher: Heraclitus of Ephesus, who surrendered his throne and became a melancholy recluse because he was distressed by human stupidity.

47 *unmannerly*: impolite, inappropriate.

48 *death's head*: skull.

51 *How . . . by*: what do you think about.

52 *pass for*: be accepted as.

55–6 *he is . . . no man*: he imitates everybody and is nobody himself.

56 *throstle*: thrush.
56–7 *falls . . . a-capering*: immediately begins to dance around.
61 *Falconbridge*: The character of this name in Shakespeare's *King John* is a model of English conduct.
65 *come . . . court*: bear witness.
66 *have . . . English*: have very little knowledge of English.
66–7 *proper man's picture*: the appearance of a handsome man.
68 *dumbshow*: mime.
suited: dressed.

69 *doublet*: sleeveless tunic.
round hose: padded breeches.
70 *behaviour*: manners.
71 *Scottish*: When James I (James VI of Scotland) came to the throne, this was discreetly changed to 'other'.
72 *neighbourly charity*: 'Charity worketh no ill to his neighbour' (Romans 13:10).
73 *borrowed . . . of*: received a blow on the ear from.
74–6 *the Frenchman . . . another*: the Frenchman also promised to repay the Englishman for another blow and added his signature and seal to the (imaginary) bond.
82–3 *fall . . . fell*: befall (= happen) . . . befell.
83 *make shift*: contrive.
84 *offer*: attempt.
85 *you . . . perform*: you would be refusing to comply with.
88 *Rhenish*: Rhineland; white wine from this district was highly esteemed.
contrary: wrong.

man in no man. If a throstle sing, he falls straight a-capering; he will fence with his own shadow. If I should marry him, I should marry twenty husbands. If he would despise me, I would forgive him; for if he love me to madness, I shall never requite him.

Nerissa
What say you then to Falconbridge, the young baron of England?

Portia
You know I say nothing to him, for he understands not me, nor I him: he hath neither Latin, French, nor Italian, and you will come into the court and swear that I have a poor penny-worth in the English. He is a proper man's picture, but alas who can converse with a dumbshow? How oddly he is suited! I think he bought his doublet in Italy, his round hose in France, his bonnet in Germany, and his behaviour everywhere.

Nerissa
What think you of the Scottish lord his neighbour?

Portia
That he hath a neighbourly charity in him, for he borrowed a box of the ear of the Englishman and swore he would pay him again when he was able. I think the Frenchman became his surety and sealed under for another.

Nerissa
How like you the young German, the Duke of Saxony's nephew!

Portia
Very vilely in the morning when he is sober, and most vilely in the afternoon when he is drunk. When he is best he is a little worse than a man, and when he is worst he is little better than a beast. And the worst fall that ever fell, I hope I shall make shift to go without him.

Nerissa
If he should offer to choose, and choose the right casket, you should refuse to perform your father's will if you should refuse to accept him.

Portia
Therefore, for fear of the worst, I pray thee set a deep glass of Rhenish wine on the contrary casket, for if the

devil be within, and the temptation without, I know he will choose it. I will do anything, Nerissa, ere I will be married to a sponge.

Nerissa

You need not fear, lady, the having any of these lords. They have acquainted me with their determinations, which is indeed to return to their home, and to trouble you with no more suit unless you may be won by some other sort than your father's imposition, depending on the caskets.

Portia

If I live to be as old as Sibylla, I will die as chaste as Diana unless I be obtained by the manner of my father's will. I am glad this parcel of wooers are so reasonable, for there is not one among them but I dote on his very absence; and I pray God grant them a fair departure.

Nerissa

Do you not remember, lady, in your father's time, a Venetian, a scholar and a soldier, that came hither in company of the Marquis of Montferrat?

Portia

Yes, yes, it was Bassanio!—as I think so was he called.

Nerissa

True, madam; he of all the men that ever my foolish eyes looked upon was the best deserving a fair lady.

Portia

I remember him well, and I remember him worthy of thy praise.

Enter a Servingman

How now, what news?

Servingman

The four strangers seek for you, madam, to take their leave; and there is a forerunner come from a fifth, the Prince of Morocco, who brings word the prince his master will be here tonight.

Portia

If I could bid the fifth welcome with so good heart as I can bid the other four farewell, I should be glad of his approach. If he have the condition of a saint, and the

92 *the having*: having to accept.

93 *determinations*: decisions.

96 *sort*: means, way.

98 *Sibylla*: In classical mythology the sibyl (= prophetess) of Cumae was granted as many years of life as she could hold grains of sand in her hand.

99 *Diana*: the classical goddess of chastity.

100 *parcel*: bunch.

104 *a scholar . . . soldier*: This was the Renaissance idea of a perfect man.

105 *Marquis of Montferrat*: The contemporary holder of this title was the Duke of Mantua, who had fought against the Turks in 1595.

106 *as I think*: Portia attempts to conceal her interest.

112 *four*: Shakespeare probably forgot that there were *six* suitors.

113 *forerunner*: herald.

118 *condition*: character, disposition.

119 *complexion*: appearance.
119–20 *I had . . . wive me*: would rather have him for a priest than a husband.
119 *shrive*: give absolution (after confession).

complexion of a devil, I had rather he should shrive me than wive me.
Come, Nerissa; sirrah, go before:
Whiles we shut the gate upon one wooer, another knocks at the door. [*Exeunt*

Act 1 Scene 3
Shylock will lend the money—but he demands an unusual bond.

SCENE 3

Venice: a public place. Enter Bassanio *with* Shylock *the Jew*

1 *ducats*: Venetian gold coins.

Shylock
Three thousand ducats, well.

Bassanio
Ay, sir, for three months.

Shylock
For three months, well.

Bassanio
For the which, as I told you, Antonio shall be bound.

5 *bound*: as security.

Shylock
Antonio shall become bound, well.

6 *stead*: supply.
pleasure: oblige.

Bassanio
May you stead me? Will you pleasure me? Shall I know your answer?

Shylock
Three thousand ducats for three months, and Antonio bound.

Bassanio
Your answer to that?

11 *good*: financially secure; but Bassanio takes the word to mean 'honourable'.

Shylock
Antonio is a good man—

Bassanio
Have you heard any imputation to the contrary?

14 *sufficient*: adequate security.
15 *in supposition*: to be assumed.
argosy: merchant ship.
17 *the Rialto*: the Venetian Stock Exchange.
19 *squandered*: scattered lavishly.

Shylock
Ho no, no, no, no: my meaning in saying he is a good man is to have you understand me that he is sufficient. Yet his means are in supposition: he hath an argosy bound to Tripolis, another to the Indies; I understand moreover upon the Rialto he hath a third at Mexico, a fourth for England, and other ventures he hath squandered abroad. But ships are but boards, sailors but

men; there be land rats, and water rats, water thieves and land thieves—I mean pirates—and then there is the peril of waters, winds, and rocks. The man is notwithstanding sufficient. Three thousand ducats: I think I may take his bond.

Bassanio

Be assured you may.

Shylock

I will be assured I may; and that I may be assured, I will bethink me—may I speak with Antonio?

Bassanio

If it please you to dine with us—

Shylock

Yes, to smell pork, to eat of the habitation which your prophet the Nazarite conjured the devil into. I will buy with you, sell with you, talk with you, walk with you, and so following; but I will not eat with you, drink with you, nor pray with you. What news on the Rialto? Who is he comes here?

Enter Antonio

Bassanio

This is Signor Antonio.

Shylock

[*Aside*] How like a fawning publican he looks!
I hate him for he is a Christian;
But more, for that in low simplicity
He lends out money gratis, and brings down
The rate of usance here with us in Venice.
If I can catch him once upon the hip,
I will feed fat the ancient grudge I bear him.
He hates our sacred nation, and he rails
Even there where merchants most do congregate
On me, my bargains, and my well-won thrift
Which he calls interest. Curs'd be my tribe
If I forgive him!

Bassanio

Shylock, do you hear?

Shylock

I am debating of my present store,

---

21 *pirates*: These were terrorists to shipping in the Adriatic.

25, 26 *assured*: a) reassured; b) financially secure.

27 *bethink me*: give the matter some consideration.

29 *pork*: A meat forbidden to the Jews.

29–30 *the habitation . . . into*: Jesus of Nazareth ('the Nazarite') ordered the devils possessing the mind of a madman to enter into a herd of pigs (St Mark 5:1–13).

32 *and so following*: etcetera.

36 *fawning publican*: servile tax-collector.

37 *for*: because.

38 *low simplicity*: humble foolishness.

39 *gratis*: interest-free.

40 *usance*: usury, money-lending.

41 *upon the hip*: at a disadvantage.

43 *rails*: speaks abuse.

45 *bargains*: business deals. *thrift*: success.

46 *interest*: profit.

48 *debating of*: reckoning up. *present store*: ready money.

And by the near guess of my memory
I cannot instantly raise up the gross
Of full three thousand ducats. What of that?
Tubal, a wealthy Hebrew of my tribe,
Will furnish me. But soft, how many months
Do you desire? [*To* Antonio] Rest you fair, good signor!
Your worship was the last man in our mouths.

Antonio

Shylock, albeit I neither lend nor borrow
By taking nor by giving of excess,
Yet to supply the ripe wants of my friend
I'll break a custom. [*To* Bassanio] Is he yet possess'd
How much ye would?

Shylock

Ay, ay, three thousand ducats.

Antonio

And for three months.

Shylock

I had forgot, three months; [*To* Bassanio] you told me so.
Well then, your bond; and let me see—but hear you,
Methoughts you said you neither lend nor borrow
Upon advantage.

Antonio

I do never use it.

Shylock

When Jacob graz'd his uncle Laban's sheep—
This Jacob from our holy Abram was
(As his wise mother wrought in his behalf)
The third possessor; ay, he was the third—

Antonio

And what of him, did he take interest?

Shylock

No, not take interest, not as you would say
Directly interest. Mark what Jacob did:
When Laban and himself were compromis'd
That all the eanlings which were streak'd and pied
Should fall as Jacob's hire, the ewes being rank
In end of autumn turned to the rams,
And when the work of generation was
Between these woolly breeders in the act,

49 *near*: close.
50 *gross*: whole sum.
53 *furnish*: supply.
soft: wait a minute.
55 *in our mouths*: that we were talking about.
56 *albeit*: although.
57 *excess*: interest, anything above the sum lent.
58 *ripe*: pressing, urgent.
59 *possess'd*: informed.
60 *would*: want.
65 *Upon advantage*: with interest.
I . . . use it: I never do so.
66–83 *When Jacob . . . Jacob's*: Shylock conflates two stories: Genesis 27 tells how Jacob, with the help of 'his wise mother', tricked his brother out of his birthright; and Genesis 30 describes the deception of Laban as Shylock recounts it here.
66 *graz'd*: shepherded.
67 *our holy Abram*: The patriarch Abraham was the founder of the Jewish race.
68 *wrought*: devised.
73 *compromis'd*: agreed.
74 *eanlings*: new-born lambs.
streak'd and pied: with fleeces of two colours.
75 *fall as Jacob's hire*: be counted as Jacob's wages.
rank: on heat, ready for mating.
76 *turned*: turnèd.
77 *work of generation*: mating.

79 *pill'd . . . wands*: went and stripped the bark of some twigs; 'me' is used purely for emphasis.
80 *deed of kind*: act of breeding.
81 *fulsome*: passionate.
82 *eaning*: lambing.
83 *Fall*: gave birth to.
85 *thrift*: profit.
86 *venture*: speculation; Antonio approves Jacob's calculated enterprise.
serv'd for: worked for; usury was condemned partly because no work was involved.
88 *sway'd*: governed.
fashion'd: shaped.
89 *Was . . . good*: did you bring up this story as a justification of usury.
93 *cite*: quote.
100 *beholding*: indebted.

101 *oft*: often.
102 *rated*: scolded.
103 *usances*: financial deals.
104 *Still*: always.
105 *suff'rance*: long-suffering, forebearance.
badge: a) characteristic; b) distinguishing mark: Venetian Jews at this time were compelled to wear a yellow O.
106 *misbeliever*: heretic, unbeliever.
dog: The Jews believed that dogs were unclean.
107 *gaberdine*: long loose coat, worn traditionally by Jews.
110 *Go to, then*: and now what are you doing (an expression of exasperation).
111 *monies*: The plural form may be Shakespeare's attempt to indicate some Jewish speech habit.
112 *void your rheum*: spit.

The skilful shepherd pill'd me certain wands
And in the doing of the deed of kind
He stuck them up before the fulsome ewes,
Who then conceiving, did in eaning time
Fall parti-coloured lambs, and those were Jacob's.
This was a way to thrive, and he was blest;
And thrift is blessing if men steal it not.

Antonio

This was a venture, sir, that Jacob serv'd for,
A thing not in his power to bring to pass,
But sway'd and fashion'd by the hand of heaven.
Was this inserted to make interest good?
Or is your gold and silver ewes and rams?

Shylock

I cannot tell, I make it breed as fast.
But note me, signor—

Antonio

Mark you this, Bassanio,
The devil can cite Scripture for his purpose.
An evil soul producing holy witness
Is like a villain with a smiling cheek,
A goodly apple rotten at the heart.
O what a goodly outside falsehood hath!

Shylock

Three thousand ducats, 'tis a good round sum.
Three months from twelve, then let me see, the rate—

Antonio

Well, Shylock, shall we be beholding to you?

Shylock

Signor Antonio, many a time and oft
In the Rialto you have rated me
About my monies and my usances.
Still have I borne it with a patient shrug
For suff'rance is the badge of all our tribe.
You call me misbeliever, cut-throat dog,
And spit upon my Jewish gaberdine,
And all for use of that which is mine own.
Well then, it now appears you need my help.
Go to, then, you come to me, and you say,
'Shylock, we would have monies'—you say so,
You that did void your rheum upon my beard,

113 *foot*: kick.

114 *suit*: request.

118 *key*: tone.

119 *With bated breath*: anxiously.

120 *Say this*: The pause in the line, allowing time for a gesture of mock-humility, throws emphasis on Shylock's conclusion.

125 *as like*: just as likely.

129 *A breed . . . friend*: an increase in the sum of sterile money from a friend.

131 *break*: go bankrupt.

136 *doit*: a Dutch coin of little value.

137 *usance*: interest.

138 *kind*: kindness; Bassanio takes the word in its normal sense—but Shylock will pun on the meaning 'natural inclination'.

140 *notary*: solicitor.
seal me: sign for me.

141 *single*: simple.
in a merry sport: as a joke.

144 *the condition*: the terms of the bond.

145 *nominated for*: named as.
equal: exact.

And foot me as you spurn a stranger cur
Over your threshold: monies is your suit.
What should I say to you? Should I not say
'Hath a dog money? Is it possible
A cur can lend three thousand ducats?' Or
Shall I bend low, and in a bondman's key,
With bated breath and whisp'ring humbleness,
Say this:
'Fair sir, you spat on me on Wednesday last,
You spurn'd me such a day, another time
You call'd me dog: and for these courtesies
I'll lend you thus much monies.'

Antonio

I am as like to call thee so again,
To spit on thee again, to spurn thee too.
If thou wilt lend this money, lend it not
As to thy friends, for when did friendship take
A breed for barren metal of his friend?
But lend it rather to thine enemy,
Who if he break, thou mayst with better face
Exact the penalty.

Shylock

Why look you how you storm!
I would be friends with you, and have your love,
Forget the shames that you have stain'd me with,
Supply your present wants, and take no doit
Of usance for my monies, and you'll not hear me.
This is kind I offer.

Bassanio

This were kindness.

Shylock

This kindness will I show.
Go with me to a notary, seal me there
Your single bond, and, in a merry sport,
If you repay me not on such a day,
In such a place, such sum or sums as are
Express'd in the condition, let the forfeit
Be nominated for an equal pound
Of your fair flesh, to be cut off and taken
In what part of your body pleaseth me.

'Yes, Shylock, I will seal unto this bond.' (*1*, 3, 167). David Suchet as Shylock and Tom Wilkinson as Antonio, Royal Shakespeare Company, 1981.

Antonio
Content, in faith! I'll seal to such a bond,
And say there is much kindness in the Jew.

Bassanio
You shall not seal to such a bond for me;
I'll rather dwell in my necessity.

Antonio
Why, fear not, man, I will not forfeit it.
Within these two months, that's a month before
This bond expires, I do expect return
Of thrice three times the value of this bond.

Shylock
O father Abram, what these Christians are,
Whose own hard dealings teaches them suspect
The thoughts of others! Pray you tell me this:
If he should break his day what should I gain
By the exaction of the forfeiture?
A pound of man's flesh, taken from a man,
Is not so estimable, profitable neither,
As flesh of muttons, beefs, or goats. I say
To buy his favour, I extend this friendship.
If he will take it, so; if not, adieu,
And for my love, I pray you wrong me not.

Antonio
Yes, Shylock, I will seal unto this bond.

Shylock
Then meet me forthwith at the notary's.
Give him direction for this merry bond,
And I will go and purse the ducats straight,
See to my house left in the fearful guard
Of an unthrifty knave, and presently
I'll be with you. [*Exit*

Antonio
Hie thee, gentle Jew.
The Hebrew will turn Christian, he grows kind.

Bassanio
I like not fair terms and a villain's mind.

Antonio
Come on, in this there can be no dismay,
My ships come home a month before the day.

[*Exeunt*

151 *dwell . . . necessity*: remain in need; Bassanio emphasizes his meaning with his rhyme.

157 *hard*: tough.
suspect: to be suspicious.

159 *break his day*: fail to pay on the agreed date.

163 *muttons, beefs*: sheep, oxen; Shylock's usage seems to emphasize his status as an 'outsider'.

170 *purse . . . straight*: get the money ready immediately.
171 *fearful*: untrustworthy.
172 *unthrifty*: careless.
knave: lad, servant.

173 *gentle*: Antonio makes a pun with 'Gentile' (= a non-Jewish person).

ACT 2

Act 2 Scene 1
Portia interviews a new suitor, and explains the conditions of her father's will.

0s.d. *flourish*: fanfare.
0s.d. *a tawny Moor . . . accordingly*: The details and the vagueness about numbers, are typical of an author's own manuscript.
accordingly: in the same way.
1–3 *Mislike . . . bred*: 'Marvel not at me that I am so black, for why? the sun hath shined upon me' (Song of Solomon).
1 *Mislike*: dislike.
2 *shadow'd*: darkened.
livery: uniform.
3 *near bred*: closely related.
4 *fairest*: most light-skinned.
5 *Phoebus*: the god of the sun.
6 *make incision*: cut ourselves.
7 *reddest*: Red blood showed courage.
8 *aspect*: aspèct.
9 *fear'd*: terrified.
10 *best-regarded*: most admired.
clime: part of the world.
12 *steal your thoughts*: win your affections.
13 *In . . . choice*: when it comes to choosing.
led: influenced.
14 *nice*: fastidious, over-particular.
16 *Bars*: forbids.
17 *scanted*: restricted.
18 *hedg'd*: confined.
18–19 *to yield . . . wife*: marry that man.
20 *renowned*: renownèd.
then . . . fair: would then have stood as good a chance; Portia plays on 'fair' = light-skinned.
21 *any comer*: any other suitor.
24 *scimitar*: short curved sword.

SCENE 1

Belmont: Portia*'s house. A flourish of cornets. Enter the* Prince of Morocco, *a tawny Moor all in white, and three or four followers accordingly; with* Portia, Nerissa, *and their train*

Morocco
Mislike me not for my complexion,
The shadow'd livery of the burnish'd sun,
To whom I am a neighbour and near bred.
Bring me the fairest creature northward born,
Where Phoebus' fire scarce thaws the icicles,
And let us make incision for your love
To prove whose blood is reddest, his or mine.
I tell thee, lady, this aspect of mine
Hath fear'd the valiant; by my love I swear
The best-regarded virgins of our clime
Have lov'd it too. I would not change this hue,
Except to steal your thoughts, my gentle queen.

Portia
In terms of choice I am not solely led
By nice direction of a maiden's eyes.
Besides, the lottery of my destiny
Bars me the right of voluntary choosing.
But if my father had not scanted me,
And hedg'd me by his wit to yield myself
His wife who wins me by that means I told you,
Yourself, renowned prince, then stood as fair
As any comer I have looked on yet
For my affection.

Morocco
Even for that I thank you.
Therefore I pray you lead me to the caskets
To try my fortune. By this scimitar,

25–6 *slew . . . Solyman*: The Moroccans owed allegiance to the Turks who, under Solyman the Magnificent, fought against the Persians in the mid-sixteenth century—but no Shah ('Sophy') was killed in the fighting.
26 *fields*: battlefields, battles.
of: over.
27 *o'er-stare*: outface, defy.
30 *a roars*: he roars.
32 *Hercules and Lichas*: In classical mythology, the superman (grandson of Alceus) and his servant.
play at dice: toss dice, gamble.
35 *So . . . rage*: just as Hercules was destroyed by his own frenzy.

That slew the Sophy and a Persian prince
That won three fields of Sultan Solyman,
I would o'er-stare the sternest eyes that look,
Outbrave the heart most daring on the earth,
Pluck the young sucking cubs from the she-bear,
Yea, mock the lion when a roars for prey,
To win thee, lady. But alas the while,
If Hercules and Lichas play at dice
Which is the better man, the greater throw
May turn by fortune from the weaker hand.
So is Alcides beaten by his rage,
And so may I, blind Fortune leading me,
Miss that which one unworthier may attain,
And die with grieving.

Portia

You must take your chance,
And either not attempt to choose at all
Or swear before you choose, if you choose wrong,
Never to speak to lady afterward
In way of marriage: therefore be advis'd.

Morocco

Nor will not. Come, bring me unto my chance.

Portia

First forward to the temple; after dinner
Your hazard shall be made.

Morocco

Good fortune then,
To make me blest—or cursed'st among men!

Cornets. [*Exeunt*

42 *In way of*: on the subject of.
be advis'd: consider, be careful.

43 *Nor will not*: I certainly won't.
chance: fate, trial.

44 *forward . . . temple*: Oaths of such magnitude were customarily taken at an altar.

46 *cursed*: cursèd.
46s.d. *Cornets*: Another fanfare to mark the Prince's departure.

Act 2 Scene 2

Lancelot Gobbo teases his blind father, who asks Bassanio to give employment to his son. Bassanio is preparing for Belmont, and Gratiano wants to accompany him.

0s.d. *Scene 2*: The action of Scenes 2–6 can be made continuous, provided that the three stage entrances are clearly identified—the door of Shylock's house, the direction of Gratiano's lodging, and the opening (perhaps the central, curtained space) for Bassanio's house.
0s.d. *the Clown*: An indication that the part was played by the company's professional comedian (Will Kemp).
1 *serve me*: a) assist me; b) obey me.
2 *The fiend*: the devil; Lancelot imagines himself as the central character of a Morality Play.
8 *scorn*: despise—with a play on the sense 'kick aside'.
9 *courageous*: encouraging.
pack: be gone.
Fia: on your way (Italian).
12 *hanging . . . heart*: clinging to my heart.
14 *honest woman*: virtuous woman.
15–16 *my father . . . taste*: Lancelot hints at his father's sexual activities.
17 *budge*: move, leave.
21 *God . . . mark*: if I may say so; Lancelot apologizes for his language.
23 *saving your reverence*: if you'll excuse me.
24 *incarnation*: incarnate; mistaken words ('malapropisms') are Will Kemp's speciality.
25 *in my conscience*: to speak truly.
26 *hard*: strict.
offer: presume.

Scene 2

Venice: the street outside Shylock*'s house. Enter* Lancelot Gobbo, *the Clown, alone*

Lancelot

Certainly, my conscience will serve me to run from this Jew my master. The fiend is at mine elbow and tempts me, saying to me 'Gobbo, Lancelot Gobbo, good Lancelot', or 'Good Gobbo', or 'Good Lancelot Gobbo, use your legs, take the start, run away.' My conscience says 'No: take heed, honest Lancelot, take heed, honest Gobbo'—or (as aforesaid)—'honest Lancelot Gobbo; do not run, scorn running with thy heels.' Well, the most courageous fiend bids me pack. 'Fia!' says the fiend, 'Away!' says the fiend. ''For the heavens, rouse up a brave mind', says the fiend, 'and run.' Well, my conscience, hanging about the neck of my heart, says very wisely to me, 'My honest friend Lancelot, being an honest man's son, or rather an honest woman's son' (for indeed my father did something smack, something grow to; he had a kind of taste): well, my conscience says 'Lancelot, budge not!' 'Budge!' says the fiend. 'Budge not!' says my conscience. 'Conscience', say I, 'you counsel well.' 'Fiend', say I, 'you counsel well'. To be ruled by my conscience, I should stay with the Jew my master who—God bless the mark!—is a kind of devil; and to run away from the Jew, I should be ruled by the fiend who—saving your reverence—is the devil himself. Certainly the Jew is the very devil incarnation, and, in my conscience, my conscience is but a kind of hard conscience to offer to counsel me to stay with the Jew. The fiend gives the more friendly counsel: I will run, fiend, my heels are at your commandment, I will run.

Enter Old Gobbo *with a basket*

Gobbo

Master young-man, you, I pray you, which is the way to Master Jew's?

'Master young-gentleman, I pray you, which is the way to Master Jew's?' (*2*, 2, 35–6). Rob Edwards as Lancelot Gobbo and Jimmy Gardner as Old Gobbo, Royal Shakespeare Company, 1981.

Lancelot

[*Aside*] O heavens! This is my true-begotten father who being more than sand-blind, high gravel-blind, knows me not. I will try confusions with him.

Gobbo

Master young-gentleman, I pray you, which is the way to Master Jew's?

Lancelot

Turn upon your right hand at the next turning, but at the next turning of all on your left. Marry, at the very next turning turn of no hand but turn down indirectly to the Jew's house.

Gobbo

Be God's sonties, 'twill be a hard way to hit! Can you tell me whether one Lancelot that dwells with him, dwell with him or no?

Lancelot

Talk you of young Master Lancelot? [*Aside*] Mark me now, now will I raise the waters. Talk you of young Master Lancelot?

Gobbo

No 'master', sir, but a poor man's son. His father, though I say't, is an honest, exceeding poor man and, God be thanked, well to live.

Lancelot

Well, let his father be what a will, we talk of young Master Lancelot.

Gobbo

Your worship's friend and Lancelot, sir.

Lancelot

But I pray you, *ergo* old man, *ergo* I beseech you, talk you of young Master Lancelot?

Gobbo

Of Lancelot, an't please your mastership.

Lancelot

Ergo Master Lancelot. Talk not of Master Lancelot, father, for the young gentleman, according to fates and destinies, and such odd sayings, the sisters three, and such branches of learning, is indeed deceased, or as you would say in plain terms, gone to heaven.

32 *true-begotten father*: Another deliberate confusion.

33 *sand-blind*: half-blind.
high . . . blind: almost stone (= completely) blind.

34 *try confusions*: test him out, give him some riddles.

37–40 *Turn . . . house*: This is an old joke, made more effective if Lancelot turns his father about until he faces Shylock's door.

38 *Marry*: by the Virgin Mary (a mild oath).

41 *Be . . . sonties*: by God's saints; Old Gobbo speaks a rural dialect.
hit: find.

42 *one*: a certain.
dwells with him: is a member of his household.

42–3 *dwell with him*: lives with him.

45 *raise the waters*: bring tears to his eyes.

49 *well to live*: well-to-do, prosperous; another malapropism.

50 *a*: he.

52 *Your . . . Lancelot*: just call him plain Lancelot.

55 *an't*: if it.

56 *ergo*: therefore; Lancelot wants to confuse his father with the Latin word.

57 *father*: A courteous way of addressing an old man—making for more comedy here.

58 *sisters three*: The Fates—three sister-goddesses of classical mythology who controlled human destiny.

Gobbo

Marry, God forbid! The boy was the very staff of my age, my very prop.

Lancelot

Do I look like a cudgel or a hovel-post, a staff or a prop? Do you know me, father?

63 *hovel-post*: main timber support of poor dwelling.

Gobbo

Alack the day, I know you not, young gentleman, but I pray you tell me, is my boy—God rest his soul!—alive or dead?

Lancelot

Do you not know me, father?

Gobbo

Alack, sir, I am sand-blind, I know you not.

Lancelot

Nay indeed, if you had your eyes you might fail of the knowing me: it is a wise father that knows his own child. Well, old man, I will tell you news of your son. [*Kneels*] Give me your blessing; truth will come to light, murder cannot be hid long, a man's son may, but in the end truth will out.

71–2 *a wise . . . child*: Lancelot inverts the proverb 'It is a wise child that knows his own father'.

Gobbo

Pray you, sir, stand up; I am sure you are not Lancelot my boy.

Lancelot

Pray you, let's have no more fooling about it, but give me your blessing; I am Lancelot your boy that was, your son that is, your child that shall be.

Gobbo

I cannot think you are my son.

Lancelot

I know not what I shall think of that; but I am Lancelot the Jew's man, and I am sure Margery your wife is my mother.

Gobbo

Her name is Margery indeed. I'll be sworn if thou be Lancelot thou art mine own flesh and blood. Lord worshipped might he be, what a beard hast thou got! Thou has got more hair on thy chin than Dobbin my fill-horse has on his tail.

88 *thou*: Old Gobbo shifts from the respectful form 'you' to the familiar form of address.

86–7 *Lord . . . be*: the Lord be praised.

87 *what . . . got*: Old Gobbo (unaware that his son is kneeling) has grasped the hair of Lancelot's head.

89 *fill-horse*: carthorse ('fills' = the shafts of a cart).

Lancelot

It should seem then that Dobbin's tail grows backward. I am sure he had more hair of his tail than I have of my face when I last saw him.

Gobbo

Lord, how art thou changed! How dost thou and thy master agree? I have brought him a present. How 'gree you now?

Lancelot

Well, well; but for mine own part, as I have set up my rest to run away, so I will not rest till I have run some ground. My master's a very Jew. Give him a present? Give him a halter! I am famished in his service; you may tell every finger I have with my ribs. Father, I am glad you are come; give me your present to one Master Bassanio, who indeed gives rare new liveries: if I serve not him, I will run as far as God has any ground. O rare fortune, here comes the man! To him, father, for I am a Jew if I serve the Jew any longer.

Enter Bassanio *with* Leonardo *and a follower or two*

Bassanio

You may do so, but let it be so hasted that supper be ready at the farthest by five of the clock. See these letters delivered, put the liveries to making, and desire Gratiano to come anon to my lodging.

[*Exit one of his men*

Lancelot

To him, father.

Gobbo

God bless your worship!

Bassanio

Gramercy; wouldst thou aught with me?

Gobbo

Here's my son, sir, a poor boy—

Lancelot

Not a poor boy, sir, but the rich Jew's man that would, sir, as my father shall specify—

90 *backward*: i.e. shorter.

91 *of*: on.

94 *agree*: suit each other.
'gree: agree.

96 *for . . . part*: so far as I am concerned.

96–7 *set . . . rest*: made up my mind; 'rest' = final gambling stake.

98 *ground*: distance.
very: real (an intensifier).

99 *halter*: rope (to hang himself).

100 *tell . . . ribs*: count all my ribs with your fingers; traditionally, Lancelot puts his father's hand on his own fingers, spread out to represent his ribs.

101 *give . . . present*: give your present on my behalf.

102 *rare new liveries*: splendid fashionable uniforms.

104–5 *a Jew*: i.e. 'someone I could not possibly be' (compare the modern 'I'm a Dutchman').

106 *hasted*: speeded up.

108 *put . . . making*: get the uniforms made.

109 *anon*: at once.

110 *To him*: speak to him.

112 *Gramercy*: may God reward you (derived from Old French *grant merci*).

116 *infection*: Gobbo's mistake for 'affection' (= desire).

118 *the short and long*: all that needs to be said; Lancelot inverts the usual phrase.

120 *saving . . . reverence*: if you'll allow me to say this.

121 *cater-cousins*: close friends who eat together.

124 *frutify*: Lancelot combines 'notify' and 'fructify' (= bear fruit)—which Old Gobbo takes as the cue for his gift.

125 *dish of doves*: doves prepared for eating.

127 *impertinent*: Lancelot means 'pertinent' (= relevant).

132 *defect*: i.e. 'effect' (= purpose).

133 *thou . . . suit*: your request is granted.

135 *preferr'd*: recommended. *preferment*: promotion.

138 *old proverb*: 'The grace of God is gear enough (for salvation)'. *parted*: divided.

142–3 *enquire . . . out*: make your way to my house.

144 *more guarded*: with more (gold) braid; the extra trimmings might suggest that Lancelot is to act as a jester.

Gobbo

He hath a great infection, sir, as one would say, to serve—

Lancelot

Indeed, the short and the long is, I serve the Jew, and have a desire, as my father shall specify—

Gobbo

His master and he, saving your worship's reverence, are scarce cater-cousins—

Lancelot

To be brief, the very truth is that the Jew having done me wrong doth cause me—as my father being I hope an old man shall frutify unto you—

Gobbo

I have here a dish of doves that I would bestow upon your worship, and my suit is—

Lancelot

In very brief, the suit is impertinent to myself, as your worship shall know by this honest old man, and though I say it, though old man, yet poor man, my father—

Bassanio

One speak for both. What would you?

Lancelot

Serve you, sir.

Gobbo

That is the very defect of the matter, sir.

Bassanio

I know thee well, thou hast obtain'd thy suit.
Shylock thy master spoke with me this day,
And hath preferr'd thee, if it be preferment
To leave a rich Jew's service to become
The follower of so poor a gentleman.

Lancelot

The old proverb is very well parted between my master Shylock and you, sir: you have the grace of God, sir, and he hath enough.

Bassanio

Thou speak'st it well; go, father, with thy son;
Take leave of thy old master, and enquire
My lodging out. [*To a follower*] Give him a livery
More guarded than his fellows'; see it done.

Lancelot

Father, in. I cannot get a service, no, I have ne'er a tongue in my head! [*Looks at palm of his hand*] Well, if any man in Italy have a fairer table which doth offer to swear upon a book!—I shall have good fortune. Go to, here's a simple line of life, here's a small trifle of wives: alas, fifteen wives is nothing, eleven widows and nine maids is a simple coming-in for one man. And then to 'scape drowning thrice, and to be in peril of my life with the edge of a featherbed: here are simple 'scapes. Well, if Fortune be a woman, she's a good wench for this gear. Father, come, I'll take my leave of the Jew in the twinkling. [*Exeunt* Lancelot *and* Gobbo

Bassanio

I pray thee, good Leonardo, think on this.
These things being bought and orderly bestow'd,
Return in haste, for I do feast tonight
My best esteem'd acquaintance. Hie thee, go.

Leonardo

My best endeavours shall be done herein.

Enter Gratiano

Gratiano

Where's your master?

Leonardo

Yonder, sir, he walks. [*Exit*

Gratiano

Signor Bassanio!

Bassanio

Gratiano?

Gratiano

I have a suit to you.

Bassanio

You have obtain'd it.

Gratiano

You must not deny me, I must go with you to Belmont.

Bassanio

Why then, you must. But hear thee, Gratiano:
Thou art too wild, too rude, and bold of voice—
Parts that become thee happily enough,

145–56 *Father . . . twinkling*: Lancelot, rejoicing with heavy irony in his success, takes his father upstage towards Shylock's door, while Bassanio and Leonardo confer downstage.
147–8 *table . . . fortune*: Lancelot pretends to read his fortune in the lines of his hand—which would be laid on the Bible to swear an oath.
148 *Go to*: come along (an expression of exasperation).
149 *simple . . . life*: straightforward lifeline (ironic).
small trifle: trivial matter.
151 *simple coming-in*: only a (sexual) beginning.
152 *'scape*: escape.
153 *'scapes*: adventures.
153–4 *if . . . woman*: Fortune is pictured as being female and fickle.
154 *gear*: business.
155–6 *in the twinkling*: in the twinkling of an eye.
158 *orderly bestow'd*: stowed neatly on board.
159 *feast*: give a banquet for.
161 *endeavours*: efforts.
165 *have . . . you*: want to ask a favour.
You . . . it: it's yours.
167 *you . . . thee*: Bassanio drops into the familiar form of address for his admonishment.
168 *rude*: uncouth, outspoken.
169 *Parts*: qualities.
become thee: suit you.

171 *show*: appear.

172 *Something too liberal*: rather too free-and-easy.
pain: care.

173 *allay*: moderate.
modesty: decorum.

174 *skipping*: boisterous, effervescent.

175 *misconster'd*: misconstrued, misinterpreted.

177 *sober habit*: a) decent costume; b) restrained behaviour.

178 *but*: only.

180 *saying*: being said.
hood: cover; Elizabethan men kept their hats on indoors, even for meals.

182 *Use . . . civility*: maintain all forms of good manners.

183 *one . . . ostent*: someone who is thoroughly accustomed to showing a serious appearance.

184 *grandam*: grandmother.

185 *bearing*: conduct.

186 *bar*: make an exception of.
gauge: measure, judge.

187 *were pity*: would be a pity.

189 *suit of mirth*: a) entertaining manner; b) party dress.

190 *purpose*: intend.

And in such eyes as ours appear not faults;
But where thou art not known, why there they show
Something too liberal. Pray thee take pain
To allay with some cold drops of modesty
Thy skipping spirit, lest through thy wild behaviour
I be misconster'd in the place I go to,
And lose my hopes.

Gratiano

Signor Bassanio, hear me:
If I do not put on a sober habit,
Talk with respect, and swear but now and then,
Wear prayer books in my pocket, look demurely,
Nay more, while grace is saying, hood mine eyes
Thus with my hat, and sigh and say 'amen',
Use all the observance of civility
Like one well studied in a sad ostent
To please his grandam, never trust me more.

Bassanio

Well, we shall see your bearing.

Gratiano

Nay, but I bar tonight, you shall not gauge me
By what we do tonight.

Bassanio

No, that were pity.
I would entreat you rather to put on
Your boldest suit of mirth, for we have friends
That purpose merriment. But fare you well,
I have some business.

Gratiano

And I must to Lorenzo and the rest;
But we will visit you at supper time. [*Exeunt*

Act 2 Scene 3
Lancelot says goodbye to Jessica, Shylock's daughter.

3 *taste*: feeling.

10 *Adieu*: goodbye (French); Lancelot's high-flown language contrasts with Jessica's simple words.
exhibit my tongue: a) inhibit me from speaking; b) express what I can't say in words.

12 *get*: get hold of, steal.

13 *something*: somewhat, rather.

15 *heinous*: monstrous, abominable.

18 *manners*: behaviour.

19 *keep promise*: keep your promise.

Scene 3

Venice: outside Shylock*'s house. Enter* Jessic
Lancelot *the Clown*

Jessica
I am sorry thou wilt leave my father so.
Our house is hell, and thou a merry devil
Didst rob it of some taste of tediousness.
But fare thee well: there is a ducat for thee.
And, Lancelot, soon at supper shalt thou see
Lorenzo, who is thy new master's guest;
Give him this letter, do it secretly.
And so farewell: I would not have my father
See me in talk with thee.

Lancelot
Adieu; tears exhibit my tongue. Most beautiful pagan, most sweet Jew, if a Christian do not play the knave and get thee, I am much deceived. But adieu; these foolish drops do something drown my manly spirit. Adieu!

[*Exit*

Jessica
Farewell, good Lancelot.
Alack, what heinous sin is it in me
To be asham'd to be my father's child!
But though I am a daughter to his blood
I am not to his manners. O Lorenzo,
If thou keep promise, I shall end this strife,
Become a Christian and thy loving wife. [*Exit*

Act 2 Scene 4
Lorenzo is planning some late-night entertainment when Lancelot brings a letter from Jessica.

1 *supper*: A meal eaten around 5.00 p.m.

2 *Disguise us*: Lorenzo is urging his friends to join him in a masque—which usually involved a spectacular entry with music and torches.

Scene 4

Venice: outside Shylock*'s house. Enter* Gratiano, Lorenzo, Salarino, *and* Solanio

Lorenzo
Nay, we will slink away in supper time,
Disguise us at my lodging, and return
All in an hour.

Gratiano
We have not made good preparation.

Salarino
We have not spoke us yet of torchbearers.

Solanio
'Tis vile unless it may be quaintly order'd,
And better in my mind not undertook.

Lorenzo
'Tis now but four of clock; we have two hours
To furnish us.

Enter Lancelot *with a letter*

Friend Lancelot! What's the news?

Lancelot
And it shall please you to break up this, it shall seem to signify.

Lorenzo
I know the hand; in faith, 'tis a fair hand,
And whiter than the paper it writ on
Is the fair hand that writ.

Gratiano
Love news, in faith!

Lancelot
By your leave, sir.

Lorenzo
Whither goest thou?

Lancelot
Marry, sir, to bid my old master the Jew to sup tonight with my new master the Christian.

Lorenzo
Hold here, take this. Tell gentle Jessica
I will not fail her; speak it privately. [*Exit* Lancelot
Go, gentlemen:
Will you prepare you for this masque tonight?
I am provided of a torchbearer.

Salarino
Ay marry, I'll be gone about it straight.

Solanio
And so will I.

Lorenzo
Meet me and Gratiano
At Gratiano's lodging some hour hence.

---

5 *spoke us*: made arrangements for.

6 *quaintly order'd*: done with style.

9 *furnish us*: get ourselves ready.

10 *And*: if.
break up: unseal.

10–11 *seem to signify*: appear to indicate.

12 *hand*: handwriting.

12, 14 *fair hand*: a) elegant handwriting; b) beautiful hand.

15 *By your leave*: please excuse me (a phrase to excuse one's departure).

17 *sup*: come to supper.

19 *this*: i.e. a tip.

23 *provided of*: supplied with.

24 *straight*: immediately.

26 *some hour*: in about an hour.

Salarino
'Tis good we do so.

[*Exeunt* Salarino *and* Solanio

Gratiano
Was not that letter from fair Jessica?

Lorenzo
I must needs tell thee all. She hath directed
How I shall take her from her father's house,
What gold and jewels she is furnish'd with,
What page's suit she hath in readiness.
If e'er the Jew her father come to heaven,
It will be for his gentle daughter's sake;
And never dare misfortune cross her foot,
Unless she do it under this excuse
That she is issue to a faithless Jew.
Come, go with me; peruse this as thou goest.
Fair Jessica shall be my torchbearer. [*Exeunt*

29 *I . . . all*: I've just got to tell you everything.
directed: instructed.
31 *furnish'd with*: in possession of.
34 *gentle*: Lorenzo seems to make a pun with 'Gentile' (see *1*, 3, 173).
35 *foot*: path.
36 *she do it*: misfortune trips her up.
under: with.
37 *issue . . . Jew*: the child of a Jew lacking Christian faith.
38 *peruse*: study.

Scene 5

Act 2 Scene 5
Shylock leaves Jessica in charge of his house.

Venice: outside Shylock*'s house. Enter* Shylock *the Jew and* Lancelot *his man that was, the Clown*

0s.d. *Clown*: i.e. the company comedian—see *2*, 2, 0s.d. note.

Shylock
Well, thou shalt see, thy eyes shall be thy judge,
The difference of old Shylock and Bassanio—
What, Jessica!—Thou shalt not gourmandize
As thou hast done with me—What, Jessica!—
And sleep, and snore, and rend apparel out.
Why, Jessica, I say!

Lancelot
Why, Jessica!

Shylock
Who bids thee call? I do not bid thee call.

Lancelot
Your worship was wont to tell me I could do nothing without bidding.

2 *of*: between.
3 *gourmandize*: gorge yourself with food.
5 *rend . . . out*: wear out your clothes by tearing them.
8 *wont*: accustomed.

Enter Jessica

Jessica
Call you? What is your will?

Shylock
I am bid forth to supper, Jessica.
There are my keys. But wherefore should I go?
I am not bid for love, they flatter me;
But yet I'll go in hate, to feed upon
The prodigal Christian. Jessica my girl,
Look to my house. I am right loath to go;
There is some ill a-brewing towards my rest,
For I did dream of money bags tonight.

Lancelot
I beseech you, sir, go; my young master doth expect your reproach.

Shylock
So do I his.

Lancelot
And they have conspired together—I will not say you shall see a masque; but if you do, then it was not for nothing that my nose fell a-bleeding on Black Monday last, at six a clock i'the morning, falling out that year on Ash Wednesday was four year in th'afternoon.

Shylock
What, are there masques? Hear you me, Jessica,
Lock up my doors, and when you hear the drum
And the vile squealing of the wry-neck'd fife,
Clamber not you up to the casements then
Nor thrust your head into the public street
To gaze on Christian fools with varnish'd faces;
But stop my house's ears—I mean my casements—
Let not the sound of shallow foppery enter
My sober house. By Jacob's staff I swear
I have no mind of feasting forth tonight:
But I will go. Go you before me, sirrah;
Say I will come.

Lancelot
I will go before, sir.
[*Aside to* Jessica] Mistress, look out at window for all this:

11 *bid forth*: invited out.
12 *wherefore*: why.

15 *prodigal*: wastrel; see *1*, 1, 129 note.
16 *Look to*: take care of.
right loath: very reluctant.
17 *There . . . rest*: something is being plotted to harm my peace of mind.
18 *tonight*: last night.
20 *reproach*: Lancelot means 'approach'—but Shylock takes his word, not his meaning.
23–6 *it . . . afternoon*: Lancelot mocks Shylock's interpretation of his dream; 'Black Monday' = Easter Monday, and 'Ash Wednesday' is the first day of Lent (40 days *before* Easter).
29 *wry-neck'd fife*: a small pipe played sideways, giving the musician a twisted ('wry') neck.
30 *casements*: windows.
32 *with . . . faces*: wearing painted masks.
34 *shallow foppery*: frivolity.
35 *Jacob's staff*: Jacob, Shylock's hero (see *1*, 3, 66–83), had only one staff when he crossed the river Jordan, yet he returned a rich man (Genesis 32:10).
36 *forth*: away from home.

41 *worth . . . eye*: The expression (= something very valuable) was proverbial; 'Jewès' is an old inflected genitive (= Jew's).

42 *Hagar's offspring*: Abraham rejected Hagar and her son (his child), who were driven into the wilderness to live as outcasts (Genesis 21:9–21).

44 *patch*: fool.

45 *profit*: learning his job.

46 *wildcat*: a nocturnal animal which rests by day.
Drones . . . me: non-working bees do not live in my beehive.

48–9 *waste . . . purse*: squander the money he has borrowed.

52 *Fast . . . find*: keep what you've got, and you'll soon get more.

54 *cross'd*: thwarted.

There will come a Christian by
With be worth a Jewès eye. [*Exit*

Shylock
What says that fool of Hagar's offspring, ha?

Jessica
His words were 'Farewell, mistress', nothing else.

Shylock
The patch is kind enough, but a huge feeder,
Snail-slow in profit, and he sleeps by day
More than the wildcat. Drones hive not with me,
Therefore I part with him, and part with him
To one that I would have him help to waste
His borrow'd purse. Well, Jessica, go in;
Perhaps I will return immediately.
Do as I bid you, shut doors after you.
Fast bind, fast find:
A proverb never stale in thrifty mind. [*Exit*

Jessica
Farewell, and if my fortune be not cross'd,
I have a father, you a daughter, lost. [*Exit*

Act 2 Scene 6
Lorenzo and his friends rescue Jessica from her father's house.

0s.d. *masquers*: Fantastic costumes, grotesque masks, and torches help to create the Carnival atmosphere that Shylock feared.

1 *penthouse*: projecting upper storey of building; Gratiano may indicate the balcony above the stage doors, or the stage roof.

5 *lovers . . . clock*: lovers always come before their time (a near-proverbial saying).

6 *Venus' pigeons*: doves drawing Venus's chariot.

7 *seal . . . made*: make sure of new engagements.

7–8 *than . . . unforfeited*: than they usually do in keeping marriage vows ('obliged faith') unbroken.

8 *obliged*: obligèd.

9 *ever holds*: is always true.

Scene 6

Venice: outside Shylock's *house. Enter the masquers,* Gratiano *and* Salarino

Gratiano
This is the penthouse under which Lorenzo
Desir'd us to make stand.

Salarino
His hour is almost past.

Gratiano
And it is marvel he outdwells his hour,
For lovers ever run before the clock.

Salarino
O, ten times faster Venus' pigeons fly
To seal love's bonds new made than they are wont
To keep obliged faith unforfeited!

Gratiano
That ever holds: who riseth from a feast
With that keen appetite that he sits down?

Where is the horse that doth untread again
His tedious measures with the unbated fire
That he did pace them first? All things that are
Are with more spirit chased than enjoy'd.
How like a younger or a prodigal
The scarfed bark puts from her native bay,
Hugg'd and embraced by the strumpet wind!
How like the prodigal doth she return
With overweather'd ribs and ragged sails,
Lean, rent, and beggar'd by the strumpet wind!

Enter Lorenzo

Salarino
Here comes Lorenzo; more of this hereafter.

Lorenzo
Sweet friends, your patience for my long abode.
Not I but my affairs have made you wait.
When you shall please to play the thieves for wives,
I'll watch as long for you then. Approach—
Here dwells my father Jew. Ho! Who's within?

Enter Jessica *above, in boy's clothes*

Jessica
Who are you? Tell me, for more certainty,
Albeit I'll swear that I do know your tongue.

Lorenzo
Lorenzo, and thy love.

Jessica
Lorenzo certain, and my love indeed,
For who love I so much? And now who knows
But you, Lorenzo, whether I am yours?

Lorenzo
Heaven and thy thoughts are witness that thou art.

Jessica
Here, catch this casket, it is worth the pains.
I am glad 'tis night, you do not look on me,
For I am much asham'd of my exchange.
But love is blind, and lovers cannot see
The pretty follies that themselves commit;

11 *untread*: retrace.
12 *measures*: steps, paces (in a riding-school display of dressage).
unbated fire: undiminished energy.
14 *chased*: chasèd.
15 *younger*: younger son.
16 *scarfed bark*: scarfèd; ship with all flags flying.
17 *embraced*: embracèd.
strumpet: unfaithful (like a prostitute).
18 *the prodigal*: The Prodigal Son wasted his inheritance on prostitutes and riotous living (see *1*, 1, 129).
19 *over-weather'd ribs*: weather-beaten timbers.
20 *rent*: torn.
22 *long abode*: staying away so long.
26 *father*: father-in-law; Lorenzo is sarcastic.
36 *exchange*: change into male clothing.

For if they could, Cupid himself would blush
To see me thus transformed to a boy.

Lorenzo

Descend, for you must be my torchbearer.

Jessica

What, must I hold a candle to my shames?
They in themselves, good sooth, are too too light.
Why, 'tis an office of discovery, love,
And I should be obscur'd.

Lorenzo

So are you, sweet,
Even in the lovely garnish of a boy.
But come at once,
For the close night doth play the runaway,
And we are stay'd for at Bassanio's feast.

Jessica

I will make fast the doors, and gild myself
With some moe ducats, and be with you straight.

[*Exit* Jessica *above*

Gratiano

Now by my hood, a gentle and no Jew!

Lorenzo

Beshrew me but I love her heartily.
For she is wise, if I can judge of her,
And fair she is, if that mine eyes be true,
And true she is, as she hath prov'd herself;
And therefore like herself, wise, fair and true,
Shall she be placed in my constant soul.

Enter Jessica

What, art thou come? On, gentleman, away!
Our masquing mates by this time for us stay.

[*Exit with* Jessica

Enter Antonio

Antonio

Who's there?

Gratiano

Signor Antonio?

---

40 *transformed*: transformèd.

43 *good sooth*: goodness knows.
light: a) apparent; b) immodest.

44 *'tis . . . discovery*: the torchbearer's job is to show light on things.

45 *obscur'd*: concealed.

46 *garnish*: costume.

48 *close*: secretive.
doth . . . runaway: is speeding by.

49 *stay'd*: waited.

50 *make fast*: lock up.
gild myself: provide myself with (more) gold.

51 *straight*: immediately.

52 *by my hood*: upon my word.
gentle: a) well-bred girl; b) Gentile.

53 *Beshrew me*: damn me (a mild oath, added for emphasis).
heartily: with all my heart.

55 *be true*: see truly.

58 *Shall . . . soul*: she will always have a place in my faithful heart.
placed: placèd.

59 *gentleman*: Lorenzo laughingly addresses Jessica in her page's costume.

'Some god direct my judgement!' (*2*, 7, 13). Sinéad Cusack as Portia and Terry Wood as Morocco, Royal Shakespeare Company, 1981.

65 *is come about*: has changed direction.
66 *presently*: immediately.
69 *to . . . sail*: to sail away.

Antonio
Fie, fie, Gratiano, where are all the rest?
'Tis nine a clock, our friends all stay for you.
No masque tonight: the wind is come about,
Bassanio presently will go aboard.
I have sent twenty out to seek for you.

Gratiano
I am glad on't; I desire no more delight
Than to be under sail and gone tonight. [*Exeunt*

Act 2 Scene 7
The Prince of Morocco examines the caskets and makes his choice.

Scene 7

Belmont: Portia*'s house. Enter* Portia *with the* Prince of Morocco *and both their trains*

1 *discover*: reveal.
2 *several*: different.

8 *as blunt*: as plain as the metal.
9 *hazard*: risk.
12 *withal*: with the casket.
14 *back again*: in reverse order.
19 *fair advantages*: good returns.
20 *dross*: rubbish, impure metal.
21 *nor . . . nor*: neither . . . nor.

Portia
Go, draw aside the curtains and discover
The several caskets to this noble prince.
Now make your choice.

Morocco
This first of gold, who this inscription bears,
'Who chooseth me, shall gain what many men desire.'
The second silver, which this promise carries,
'Who chooseth me, shall get as much as he deserves.'
This third dull lead, with warning all as blunt,
'Who chooseth me, must give and hazard all he hath.'
How shall I know if I do choose the right?

Portia
The one of them contains my picture, prince.
If you choose that, then I am yours withal.

Morocco
Some god direct my judgement! Let me see:
I will survey th'inscriptions back again.
What says this leaden casket?
'Who chooseth me, must give and hazard all he hath.'
Must give—for what? For lead? Hazard for lead!
This casket threatens: men that hazard all
Do it in hope of fair advantages.
A golden mind stoops not to shows of dross;
I'll then nor give nor hazard aught for lead.
What says the silver with her virgin hue?

25 *even*: impartial.
26 *rated*: judged.
estimation: reputation.
29 *afear'd . . . deserving*: unsure what I deserve.
30 *disabling*: belittling.
36 *grav'd*: engraved.
40 *mortal breathing*: living.
41 *Hyrcanian deserts*: The classical name for a savage region south of the Caspian Sea.
vasty wilds: immense wildernesses.
42 *throughfares*: main roads.
44 *The watery kingdom*: Neptune's realm, the ocean.
44–5 *whose . . . heaven*: whose waves surge up to the sky.
45 *bar*: obstacle.
46 *spirits*: men of courage.
49 *like*: likely.
50–1 *it were . . . cerecloth*: lead would be too coarse to enfold the shroud.
51 *obscure*: dark; the emphasis is on the first syllable.
52 *immur'd*: walled in.
53 *ten . . . gold*: of ten times less value than pure ('tried') gold.
54–5 *Never . . . gold*: jewels as precious as Portia are never set in anything but gold.
56 *A coin . . . angel*: The coin, called an 'angel', depicted the archangel Michael.
57 *Stamped*: stampèd.
insculp'd upon: engraved.
61 *form*: picture.

'Who chooseth me, shall get as much as he deserves.'
As much as he deserves—pause there, Morocco,
And weigh thy value with an even hand.
If thou be'st rated by thy estimation
Thou dost deserve enough; and yet enough
May not extend so far as to the lady;
And yet to be afear'd of my deserving
Were but a weak disabling of myself.
As much as I deserve: why, that's the lady.
I do in birth deserve her, and in fortunes,
In graces, and in qualities of breeding:
But more than these, in love I do deserve.
What if I stray'd no farther, but chose here?
Let's see once more this saying grav'd in gold:
'Who chooseth me, shall gain what many men desire.'
Why, that's the lady; all the world desires her.
From the four corners of the earth they come
To kiss this shrine, this mortal breathing saint.
The Hyrcanian deserts and the vasty wilds
Of wide Arabia are as throughfares now
For princes to come view fair Portia.
The watery kingdom, whose ambitious head
Spits in the face of heaven, is no bar
To stop the foreign spirits, but they come
As o'er a brook to see fair Portia.
One of these three contains her heavenly picture.
Is't like that lead contains her? 'Twere damnation
To think so base a thought; it were too gross
To rib her cerecloth in the obscure grave.
Or shall I think in silver she's immur'd,
Being ten times undervalu'd to tried gold?
O sinful thought! Never so rich a gem
Was set in worse than gold. They have in England
A coin that bears the figure of an angel
Stamped in gold; but that's insculp'd upon:
But here an angel in a golden bed
Lies all within. Deliver me the key:
Here do I choose, and thrive I as I may.

Portia
There take it, prince, and if my form lie there,
Then I am yours.

Morocco unlocks the gold casket

Morocco

O hell! What have we here?
A carrion death, within whose empty eye
There is a written scroll. I'll read the writing.
'All that glisters is not gold;
Often have you heard that told.
Many a man his life hath sold
But my outside to behold.
Gilded tombs do worms infold.
Had you been as wise as bold,
Young in limbs, in judgement old,
Your answer had not been inscroll'd.
Fare you well, your suit is cold.'
Cold indeed, and labour lost;
Then farewell heat, and welcome frost.
Portia, adieu; I have too griev'd a heart
To take a tedious leave: thus losers part.

[*Exit* Morocco *with his train*

Portia

A gentle riddance! Draw the curtains, go.
Let all of his complexion choose me so. [*Exeunt*

A flourish of cornets

63 *A carrion death*: a death's-head, a skull.

65 *glisters*: glitters.
72 *Your . . . inscroll'd*: you would not have got the answer on this scroll.
73 *your . . . cold*: your hopes are dead.

79 *of his complexion*: like him.

Scene 8

Act 2 Scene 8
Salarino and Solanio gossip about the news: Lorenzo is missing, Shylock has been robbed, and Antonio is in trouble.

Venice: a street. Enter Salarino *and* Solanio

Salarino

Why, man, I saw Bassanio under sail,
With him is Gratiano gone along;
And in their ship I am sure Lorenzo is not.

Solanio

The villain Jew with outcries rais'd the duke,
Who went with him to search Bassanio's ship.

Salarino

He came too late, the ship was under sail.
But there the duke was given to understand

1 *under sail*: sail away.

4 *rais'd*: roused.

8 *gondola*: a flat-bottomed boat used on the canals of Venice.

10 *certified*: assured.

18 *sealed*: sealèd.

19 *double ducats*: worth double the value of ducats.

24 *his stones*: a) jewels; b) testicles.

25 *look . . . day*: be sure to pay his debt on the appointed day.

28 *reason'd*: spoke.

29 *the Narrow Seas*: the English Channel.

30 *miscarried*: miscarrièd; perished.

31 *fraught*: laden.

That in a gondola were seen together
Lorenzo and his amorous Jessica.
Besides, Antonio certified the duke
They were not with Bassanio in his ship.

Solanio

I never heard a passion so confus'd,
So strange, outrageous, and so variable,
As the dog Jew did utter in the streets:
'My daughter! O my ducats! O my daughter!
Fled with a Christian! O my Christian ducats!
Justice! The law! My ducats and my daughter!
A sealed bag, two sealed bags of ducats,
Of double ducats, stolen from me by my daughter!
And jewels—two stones, two rich and precious stones,
Stolen by my daughter! Justice! Find the girl!
She hath the stones upon her and the ducats!'

Salarino

Why, all the boys in Venice follow him,
Crying his stones, his daughter, and his ducats.

Solanio

Let good Antonio look he keep his day,
Or he shall pay for this.

Salarino

Marry, well remember'd:
I reason'd with a Frenchman yesterday
Who told me, in the Narrow Seas that part
The French and English, there miscarried
A vessel of our country richly fraught.
I thought upon Antonio when he told me,
And wish'd in silence that it were not his.

40 *Slubber not business*: don't be hurried and careless with your affairs.

41 *stay . . . time*: wait until the time is exactly right.

42 *for*: as for.

43 *mind of love*: love-schemes.

45 *ostents*: demonstrations.

46 *conveniently become you*: make you appropriately attractive.

47 *even there*: just at that point.

49 *affection . . . sensible*: amazingly powerful emotion.

51 *he . . . him*: Bassanio is all he lives for.

53 *quicken . . . heaviness*: brighten up this misery that he's indulging in. *embraced*: embracèd.

Solanio

You were best to tell Antonio what you hear.
Yet do not suddenly, for it may grieve him.

Salarino

A kinder gentleman treads not the earth.
I saw Bassanio and Antonio part:
Bassanio told him he would make some speed
Of his return: he answered, 'Do not so.
Slubber not business for my sake, Bassanio,
But stay the very riping of the time;
And for the Jew's bond which he hath of me,
Let it not enter in your mind of love.
Be merry, and employ your chiefest thoughts
To courtship, and such fair ostents of love
As shall conveniently become you there.'
And even there, his eye being big with tears,
Turning his face, he put his hand behind him,
And with affection wondrous sensible
He wrung Bassanio's hand, and so they parted.

Solanio

I think he only loves the world for him.
I pray thee let us go and find him out
And quicken his embraced heaviness
With some delight or other.

Salarino

Do we so. [*Exeunt*

Act 2 Scene 9

Another suitor makes his choice—and Portia learns that Bassanio is coming to Belmont.

0s.d. *Servitor*: servingman.

1 *draw*: pull back. *straight*: immediately.

3 *to his election*: to make his choice.

Scene 9

Belmont: Portia*'s house. Enter* Nerissa *and a* Servitor

Nerissa

Quick, quick, I pray thee, draw the curtain straight.
The Prince of Arragon hath tane his oath,
And comes to his election presently.

A flourish of cornets. Enter the Prince of Arragon*, his train, and* Portia

Portia

Behold, there stand the caskets, noble prince.

If you choose that wherein I am contain'd,
Straight shall our nuptial rites be solemniz'd;
But if you fail, without more speech, my lord,
You must be gone from hence immediately.

Arragon

I am enjoin'd by oath to observe three things:
First, never to unfold to anyone
Which casket 'twas I chose; next, if I fail
Of the right casket, never in my life
To woo a maid in way of marriage; lastly,
If I do fail in fortune of my choice,
Immediately to leave you and be gone.

Portia

To these injunctions everyone doth swear
That comes to hazard for my worthless self.

Arragon

And so have I address'd me. Fortune now
To my heart's hope! Gold, silver, and base lead.
'Who chooseth me, must give and hazard all he hath.'
You shall look fairer ere I give or hazard.
What says the golden chest? Ha, let me see:
'Who chooseth me, shall gain what many men desire.'
What many men desire: that 'many' may be meant
By the fool multitude that choose by show,
Not learning more than the fond eye doth teach,
Which pries not to th'interior, but like the martlet
Builds in the weather on the outward wall,
Even in the force and road of casualty.
I will not choose what many men desire,
Because I will not jump with common spirits,
And rank me with the barbarous multitudes.
Why then, to thee, thou silver treasure house:
Tell me once more what title thou dost bear.
'Who chooseth me, shall get as much as he deserves.'
And well said too, for who shall go about
To cozen Fortune and be honourable
Without the stamp of merit? Let none presume
To wear an undeserved dignity.
O, that estates, degrees, and offices
Were not deriv'd corruptly, and that clear honour
Were purchas'd by the merit of the wearer!

6 *solemniz'd*: performed.

9 *enjoin'd*: bound.
observe: promise.
10 *unfold*: disclose.

14 *do . . . choice*: make an unlucky choice.

17 *hazard*: gamble.

18 *address'd me*: prepared myself (by taking the oath).
Fortune: good luck.

24–5 *be . . . By*: refer to.
25 *show*: appearance.
26 *fond*: foolish.
27 *pries not*: doesn't look into.
the martlet: the swift, or house-martin.
28 *Builds . . . weather*: builds its nest exposed to the weather.
29 *Even . . . casualty*: right in the power and path of destruction.
31 *jump*: go along with.
32 *rank me*: class myself.
36–7 *go . . . cozen*: try to cheat.
38 *Without . . . merit*: without the legal authorization ('stamp') of merit.
39 *wear*: hold; positions of rank and authority are usually indicated by the wearing of some badge or garment.
undeserved: undeservèd.
40 *estates . . . offices*: estates of the realm (e.g. nobility), ranks within these estates (e.g. earls, barons), and official appointments (e.g. the chancellorship).
41 *deriv'd*: obtained.
42 *the wearer*: the bearer.

How many then should cover that stand bare!
How many be commanded that command!
How much low peasantry would then be glean'd
From the true seed of honour, and how much honour
Pick'd from the chaff and ruin of the times
To be new varnish'd! Well, but to my choice.
'Who chooseth me, shall get as much as he deserves.'
I will assume desert. Give me a key for this,
And instantly unlock my fortunes here.

Arragon unlocks the silver casket

Portia
Too long a pause for that which you find there.

Arragon
What's here? The portrait of a blinking idiot
Presenting me a schedule! I will read it.
How much unlike art thou to Portia!
How much unlike my hopes and my deservings.
'Who chooseth me, shall have as much as he deserves.'
Did I deserve no more than a fool's head?
Is that my prize? Are my deserts no better?

Portia
To offend and judge are distinct offices,
And of opposed natures.

Arragon
What is here?
[*He reads*] 'The fire seven times tried this;
Seven times tried that judgement is
That did never choose amiss.
Some there be that shadows kiss;
Such have but a shadow's bliss.
There be fools alive iwis
Silver'd o'er, and so was this.
Take what wife you will to bed,
I will ever be your head.
So be gone, you are sped.'
Still more fool I shall appear
By the time I linger here.
With one fool's head I came to woo,
But I go away with two.

43 *cover*: keep their hats on (instead of doffing them in respect to superiors).

45 *glean'd*: picked out.

47 *Pick'd . . . times*: sorted out from what the modern age rejects and spoils.

48 *new varnish'd*: a) polished up (like grains of corn); b) newly-painted (as a coat-of-arms).

50 *I will . . . desert*: I will claim to be deserving ('assume' = put on the ceremonial insignia of).

52 *Too . . . pause*: Arragon is speechless.

53 *blinking*: goggle-eyed.

54 *schedule*: written scroll.

60–1 *To . . . natures*: Portia cannot comment on the offence she has (unwittingly) given Arragon.

61 *opposed*: opposèd.

62 *The . . . this*: this silver was tested seven times in the furnace.

64 *amiss*: wrongly.

65 *shadows kiss*: embrace illusions.

67 *iwis*: assuredly.

68 *Silver'd o'er*: covered in silver (with decorations, or with white hair).

69–70 *Take . . . head*: whatever wife you marry, you will always be a fool.

71 *sped*: finished.

72–3 *Still . . . here*: I shall appear an even bigger fool the longer I stay here.

Sweet, adieu; I'll keep my oath,
Patiently to bear my wroth.
[*Exit* Arragon *with his train*

Portia
Thus hath the candle singed the moth.
O, these deliberate fools! When they do choose
They have the wisdom by their wit to lose.

Nerissa
The ancient saying is no heresy:
'Hanging and wiving goes by destiny.'

Portia
Come draw the curtain, Nerissa.

Enter a Messenger

Messenger
Where is my lady?

Portia
Here. What would my lord?

Messenger
Madam, there is alighted at your gate
A young Venetian, one that comes before
To signify th'approaching of his lord,
From whom he bringeth sensible regreets:
To wit, besides commends and courteous breath,
Gifts of rich value. Yet I have not seen
So likely an ambassador of love.
A day in April never came so sweet
To show how costly summer was at hand
As this forespurrer comes before his lord.

Portia
No more I pray thee, I am half afear'd
Thou wilt say anon he is some kin to thee,
Thou spend'st such highday wit in praising him.
Come, come, Nerissa, for I long to see
Quick Cupid's post that comes so mannerly.

Nerissa
Bassanio, Lord Love, if thy will it be! [*Exeunt*

77 *wroth*: A possible spelling of either 'ruth' (= grief), or 'wrath'.

78 *singed*: burnt.

79 *deliberate*: reasoning, debating.

80 *They . . . lose*: their reasoning ('wit') gives them the wisdom to make the wrong choice.

81 *The . . . heresy*: the old proverb was no mistaken belief.

82 *wiving*: marrying.

84 *what . . . lord*: what do you want (Portia is ironic).

85 *alighted*: landed, dismounted.

87 *signify*: announce.

88 *sensible regreets*: tangible greetings (i.e. gifts).

89 *commends . . . breath*: compliments and polite speeches.

91 *likely*: a) promising; b) handsome.

92 *A day in April*: In England.

93 *costly*: rich (in flowers).
at hand: near.

94 *forespurrer*: herald (who spurs his horse ahead of the main party).

95 *afear'd*: afraid.

96 *anon*: presently.

97 *highday wit*: well-dressed language.

99 *post*: messenger.
mannerly: courteously.

100 *Bassanio . . . be*: O Lord Love, let it be Bassanio.

ACT 3

Act 3 Scene 1
Trouble for Antonio: Shylock rejoices in his power over the merchant—and laments for the loss of his daughter.

SCENE 1

Venice: a street. Enter Solanio *and* Salarino

Solanio
Now, what news on the Rialto?

Salarino
Why, yet it lives there unchecked that Antonio hath a ship of rich lading wrecked on the Narrow Seas; the Goodwins I think they call the place—a very dangerous flat, and fatal, where the carcasses of many a tall ship lie buried, as they say, if my gossip Report be an honest woman of her word.

Solanio
I would she were as lying a gossip in that as ever knapped ginger or made her neighbours believe she wept for the death of a third husband. But it is true, without any slips of prolixity, or crossing the plain highway of talk, that the good Antonio, the honest Antonio—O that I had a title good enough to keep his name company!—

Salarino
Come, the full stop.

Solanio
Ha, what sayest thou? Why, the end is, he hath lost a ship.

Salarino
I would it might prove the end of his losses.

Solanio
Let me say 'amen' betimes, lest the devil cross my prayer, for here he comes in the likeness of a Jew.

Enter Shylock

How now, Shylock, what news among the merchants?

2 *it lives*: the rumour persists.
unchecked: without contradiction.
3 *lading*: loading, cargo.
the Narrow Seas: the English Channel.
4 *the Goodwins*: The Goodwin Sands in the middle of the Channel are a major hazard for shipping.
5 *flat*: sandbank.
tall: fine.
6 *my gossip Report*: my old friend Rumour ('gossip' = godmother).
8 *in that*: in that report.
9 *knapped*: munched; ginger (also associated with old women in *Measure for Measure*, *4*, 3, 7) is good for flatulence.
11–12 *without . . . talk*: without falling into garrulousness or deviating from a straightforward account; Solanio illustrates the fault he claims to avoid.
15 *Come . . . stop*: a) finish your sentence; b) rein in your horse (from a full gallop).
19 *betimes*: quickly.
cross: a) frustrate; b) sign with a cross.

Shylock
You knew, none so well, none so well as you, of my daughter's flight.

Salarino
That's certain; I for my part knew the tailor that made the wings she flew withal.

Solanio
And Shylock for his own part knew the bird was fledged, and then it is the complexion of them all to leave the dam.

Shylock
She is damned for it.

Salarino
That's certain—if the devil may be her judge.

Shylock
My own flesh and blood to rebel!

Solanio
Out upon it, old carrion! Rebels it at these years?

Shylock
I say my daughter is my flesh and my blood.

Salarino
There is more difference between thy flesh and hers than between jet and ivory; more between your bloods than there is between red wine and Rhenish. But tell us, do you hear whether Antonio have had any loss at sea or no?

Shylock
There I have another bad match: a bankrupt, a prodigal, who dare scarce show his head on the Rialto, a beggar that was used to come so smug upon the mart. Let him look to his bond. He was wont to call me usurer; let him look to his bond. He was wont to lend money for a Christian courtesy; let him look to his bond.

Salarino
Why, I am sure if he forfeit thou wilt not take his flesh. What's that good for?

Shylock
To bait fish withal; if it will feed nothing else, it will feed my revenge. He hath disgraced me, and hindered me half a million, laughed at my losses, mocked at my gains, scorned my nation, thwarted my bargains, cooled

25 *withal*: with.

27 *fledged*: had feathers.
complexion: nature, disposition.

28 *dam*: mother.

30 *the devil*: i.e. Shylock himself.

32 *Out . . . carrion*: get away with you, you dirty old man; Solanio pretends that Shylock is referring to his own body.

36 *Rhenish*: expensive white German wine.

39 *match*: bargain.

41 *smug*: pleased with himself.
mart: stock exchange.

42 *look to*: take care of.
wont: accustomed.

43–4 *for . . . courtesy*: out of Christian charity.

47 *bait*: use as a bait for.

48 *disgraced*: done me disfavour.

48–9 *hindered . . . million*: prevented me from making half a million ducats profit.

50 *bargains*: business deals.
cooled: alienated.

my friends, heated mine enemies—and what's his reason? I am a Jew. Hath not a Jew eyes? Hath not a Jew hands, organs, dimensions, senses, affections, passions? Fed with the same food, hurt with the same weapons, subject to the same diseases, healed by the same means, warmed and cooled by the same winter and summer as a Christian is? If you prick us, do we not bleed? If you tickle us, do we not laugh? If you poison us, do we not die? And if you wrong us, shall we not revenge? If we are like you in the rest, we will resemble you in that. If a Jew wrong a Christian, what is his humility? Revenge. If a Christian wrong a Jew, what should his sufferance be by Christian example? Why, revenge! The villainy you teach me I will execute, and it shall go hard but I will better the instruction.

Enter a Servingman *from* Antonio

Servingman
Gentlemen, my master Antonio is at his house, and desires to speak with you both.

Salarino
We have been up and down to seek him.

Enter Tubal

Solanio
Here comes another of the tribe; a third cannot be matched, unless the devil himself turn Jew.

[*Exeunt* Salarino *and* Solanio *with the* Servingman

Shylock
How now, Tubal, what news from Genoa? Hast thou found my daughter?

Tubal
I often came where I did hear of her, but cannot find her.

Shylock
Why there, there, there, there! A diamond gone cost me two thousand ducats in Frankfurt! The curse never fell upon our nation till now, I never felt it till now. Two thousand ducats in that, and other precious, precious

51 *heated*: enraged.

53 *dimensions*: bodily parts, limbs. *affections, passions*: Elizabethan psychology distinguished between 'affections' (= strong sensuous responses of attraction or revulsion) and 'passions' (= disturbances of the mind).

61 *what . . . humility*: what is the response of his Christian humility.

62 *sufferance*: forebearance (see *1*, 3, 105).

64–5 *it . . . instruction*: unless something serious prevents me, I will improve on what you have taught me.

68 *up . . . him*: looking everywhere for him.

69–70 *cannot be matched*: cannot be found to equal these two.

76 *Frankfurt*: A great jewel fair was held here annually.

76–7 *The . . . nation*: The Jews were cursed and condemned to eternal exile because they disobeyed God's law (Daniel 9:11).

jewels! I would my daughter were dead at my foot, and the jewels in her ear: would she were hearsed at my foot, and the ducats in her coffin. No news of them, why so? And I know not what's spent in the search. Why thou loss upon loss—the thief gone with so much, and so much to find the thief, and no satisfaction, no revenge, nor no ill luck stirring but what lights o'my shoulders, no sighs but o'my breathing, no tears but o'my shedding!

Tubal

Yes, other men have ill luck too. Antonio as I heard in Genoa—

Shylock

What, what, what? Ill luck, ill luck?

Tubal

—hath an argosy cast away coming from Tripolis.

Shylock

I thank God, I thank God. Is it true, is it true?

Tubal

I spoke with some of the sailors that escaped the wreck.

Shylock

I thank thee, good Tubal: good news, good news! Ha, ha, heard in Genoa!

Tubal

Your daughter spent in Genoa, as I heard, one night four score ducats.

Shylock

Thou stick'st a dagger in me; I shall never see my gold again. Four score ducats at a sitting! Four score ducats!

Tubal

There came divers of Antonio's creditors in my company to Venice that swear he cannot choose but break.

Shylock

I am very glad of it. I'll plague him, I'll torture him. I am glad of it.

Tubal

One of them showed me a ring that he had of your daughter for a monkey.

80 *hearsed*: laid in her coffin.

82–3 *Why . . . loss*: Shylock's angry grief makes him inarticulate.

85 *lights o'*: lands upon.

86 *but o'my breathing*: except those I sigh.

91 *argosy*: trading vessel.
cast away: wrecked.

96 *one night*: in one night.

99 *at a sitting*: on a single occasion.

100 *divers*: several.
100–1 *in my company*: along with me.

102 *break*: go bankrupt.

105 *of*: from.

107 *Out upon her*: A common expression of impatience.
108 *had it of Leah*: it was a present from Leah; Shylock's wife is presumably dead.
110 *undone*: ruined.
111–12 *fee . . . officer*: hire a sheriff's officer at my expense (to arrest Antonio).
112 *bespeak . . . before*: order him to be ready two weeks before the debt's repayment is due.
114 *make . . . will*: drive whatever bargains I like.
115 *synagogue*: The Jewish moneylenders will confirm their dealings with an oath.

Shylock

Out upon her! Thou torturest me, Tubal: it was my turquoise, I had it of Leah when I was a bachelor. I would not have given it for a wilderness of monkeys.

Tubal

But Antonio is certainly undone.

Shylock

Nay, that's true, that's very true. Go, Tubal, fee me an officer, bespeak him a fortnight before. I will have the heart of him if he forfeit, for were he out of Venice I can make what merchandise I will. Go, Tubal, and meet me at our synagogue, go, good Tubal, at our synagogue, Tubal. [*Exeunt*

Act 3 Scene 2
Bassanio makes his choice of caskets, winning Portia for his wife. Nerissa agrees to marry Gratiano, and both contracts are sealed with a ring. Lorenzo and Jessica arrive in Belmont, bringing a letter from Antonio.

0s.d. *trains*: attendants.
1 *tarry*: delay.
2 *hazard*: take the risk.
5 *I would not*: I don't want to.
6 *Hate . . . quality*: hatred does not give advice in this manner.
8 *a maiden . . . thought*: maidenly modesty won't let me speak my thoughts.
10 *venture for me*: try to win me.
11 *am forsworn*: have broken my vow.
12 *miss*: lose.

Scene 2

Belmont: Portia*'s house. Enter* Bassanio, Portia, Gratiano, Nerissa, *and all their trains*

Portia

I pray you tarry, pause a day or two
Before you hazard, for in choosing wrong
I lose your company; therefore forbear a while.
There's something tells me, but it is not love,
I would not lose you; and you know yourself
Hate counsels not in such a quality.
But lest you should not understand me well—
And yet a maiden hath no tongue but thought—
I would detain you here some month or two
Before you venture for me. I could teach you
How to choose right, but then I am forsworn.
So will I never be. So may you miss me;

13–14 *wish . . . forsworn*: wish I had sinned and broken my vow.
14 *Beshrew*: a curse upon.
15 *o'erlook'd*: bewitched.

18–19 *these . . . rights*: these wicked times bar owners from claiming what belongs to them.
20 *Prove it so*: if it happens that I am lost to you.
21 *Let . . . hell*: let Fortune go to hell for depriving you of what is yours.
22 *peize*: weigh down, prolong.
23 *eche it*: stretch it out.
24 *stay . . . election*: hold you back from making a choice.

25 *the rack*: an instrument of torture, stretching out the victim's body (as Portia is trying to stretch out the time) until he confessed his treason.

28 *mistrust*: anxiety.
29 *fear . . . love*: afraid that I shall not be able to have you as my wife.
30 *amity*: friendship.

33 *enforced*: enforcèd; compelled (by torture).

36 *Had . . . confession*: would have been my full confession.

38 *deliverance*: release.

42 *aloof*: at a distance, upstage.

But if you do, you'll make me wish a sin,
That I had been forsworn. Beshrew your eyes!
They have o'erlook'd me and divided me:
One half of me is yours, the other half yours—
Mine own, I would say: but if mine then yours,
And so all yours. O these naughty times
Puts bars between the owners and their rights!
And so though yours, not yours. Prove it so,
Let Fortune go to hell for it, not I.
I speak too long, but 'tis to peize the time,
To eche it, and to draw it out in length,
To stay you from election.

Bassanio

Let me choose,
For as I am, I live upon the rack.

Portia

Upon the rack, Bassanio? Then confess
What treason there is mingl'd with your love.

Bassanio

None but that ugly treason of mistrust
Which makes me fear th'enjoying of my love.
There may as well be amity and life
'Tween snow and fire, as treason and my love.

Portia

Ay, but I fear you speak upon the rack
Where men enforced do speak anything.

Bassanio

Promise me life and I'll confess the truth.

Portia

Well then, confess and live.

Bassanio

'Confess and love'
Had been the very sum of my confession.
O happy torment, when my torturer
Doth teach me answers for deliverance!
But let me to my fortune and the caskets.

Portia

Away then! I am lock'd in one of them:
If you do love me, you will find me out.
Nerissa and the rest, stand all aloof.
Let music sound while he doth make his choice;

44 *swan-like end*: It was an old belief that the mute swan sang once before its death.
45 *Fading*: dying, vanishing away.
46 *stand . . . proper*: fit more exactly.
46–7 *my eye . . . him*: I shall weep, and he will seem to drown in my tears.
49 *flourish*: trumpet fanfare.
50 *crowned*: crownèd.
51 *dulcet*: sweet.
54 *presence*: noble bearing.
55 *Alcides*: Hercules (grandson of Alceus) rescued a Trojan princess, Hesione, who was being sacrificed to a sea-monster.
56 *howling*: lamenting.
57 *I . . . sacrifice*: I represent the sacrificial victim.
58 *Dardanian wives*: Trojan women; Dardanus was the legendary founder of Troy.
59 *bleared visages*: blearèd; tear-stained faces.
60 *issue*: outcome.
61 *Live thou*: if you live.
62 *fray*: fighting.
62s.d. *comments . . . himself*: ponders silently over the caskets; the words of the song seem to articulate his thoughts.
63 *fancy*: attraction.
64 *Or . . . or*: either . . . or.
65 *nourished*: nourishèd.
67 *engend'red*: generated.
69 *in the cradle*: i.e. in its infancy.
70 *knell*: funeral bell.
73 *shows*: appearances.
least themselves: not what they are.
74 *still*: continually.
76 *season'd . . . voice*: presented with eloquence (like rotten food disguised with spices).
78 *damned error*: damnèd; heresy, false belief.
sober brow: solemn-faced person.

Then if he lose he makes a swan-like end,
Fading in music. That the comparison
May stand more proper, my eye shall be the stream
And watery deathbed for him. He may win,
And what is music then? Then music is
Even as the flourish when true subjects bow
To a new-crowned monarch. Such it is
As are those dulcet sounds in break of day,
That creep into the dreaming bridegroom's ear
And summon him to marriage. Now he goes
With no less presence, but with much more love,
Than young Alcides when he did redeem
The virgin tribute paid by howling Troy
To the sea-monster. I stand for sacrifice.
The rest aloof are the Dardanian wives,
With bleared visages come forth to view
The issue of th'exploit. Go, Hercules!
Live thou, I live. With much much more dismay
I view the fight than thou that mak'st the fray.

Here music. A song the whilst Bassanio *comments on the caskets to himself*

Tell me where is fancy bred,
Or in the heart, or in the head?
How begot, how nourished?
  Reply, reply.
It is engend'red in the eye,
With gazing fed, and fancy dies
In the cradle where it lies.
Let us all ring fancy's knell.
I'll begin it—Ding, dong, bell.

All

Ding, dong, bell.

Bassanio

So may the outward shows be least themselves:
The world is still deceiv'd with ornament.
In law, what plea so tainted and corrupt
But, being season'd with a gracious voice,
Obscures the show of evil? In religion,
What damned error but some sober brow

79 *approve . . . text*: confirm it with a quotation from the Bible (see *1*, 3, 93).

81 *simple*: a) uncomplicated; b) foolish.

84 *stayers*: ropes; many editions have 'stairs' (= sandbanks).
yet: nevertheless.

85 *Hercules . . . Mars*: the superman and the god of war in classical mythology.

86 *inward search'd*: intestinally examined.
livers . . . milk: The liver, believed to be the seat of courage, should be red with blood.

87 *valour's excrement*: the outgrowth of a brave man—i.e. a beard.

88 *redoubted*: terrible, fearsome.

89 *purchas'd . . . weight*: Cosmetics and false hair (taken from dead bodies or from prostitutes) could be bought by the kilo.

91 *lightest*: a) most dissolute; b) most light-weight (morally).

92 *crisped*: crispèd; curled.
snaky: flowing.

93 *wanton*: promiscuous.

94 *supposed fairness*: supposèd; presumed beauty.

95 *dowry*: endowment, gift.

97 *guiled*: guilèd; treacherous.

99 *Indian beauty*: A contradiction in terms: Elizabethans thought there was beauty only in fair skins.

102 *Hard . . . Midas*: Food became a problem when Apollo granted the mythological king's wish that all he touched might turn to gold.

103 *common drudge*: general servant.

106 *paleness*: lack of colour.

109 *As*: such as.

110 *green-ey'd jealousy*: Compare the proverbial 'green with envy'.

111 *allay*: diminish.

112 *measure*: moderation.
scant: restrain.

Will bless it and approve it with a text,
Hiding the grossness with fair ornament?
There is no vice so simple but assumes
Some mark of virtue on his outward parts.
How many cowards whose hearts are all as false
As stayers of sand, wear yet upon their chins
The beards of Hercules and frowning Mars,
Who inward search'd have livers white as milk,
And these assume but valour's excrement
To render them redoubted. Look on beauty,
And you shall see 'tis purchas'd by the weight,
Which therein works a miracle in nature,
Making them lightest that wear most of it.
So are those crisped snaky golden locks
Which maketh such wanton gambols with the wind
Upon supposed fairness, often known
To be the dowry of a second head,
The skull that bred them in the sepulchre.
Thus ornament is but the guiled shore
To a most dangerous sea; the beauteous scarf
Veiling an Indian beauty; in a word,
The seeming truth which cunning times put on
To entrap the wisest. Therefore thou gaudy gold,
Hard food for Midas, I will none of thee,
Nor none of thee, thou pale and common drudge
'Tween man and man. But thou, thou meagre lead
Which rather threaten'st than dost promise aught,
Thy paleness moves me more than eloquence:
And here choose I. Joy be the consequence!

Portia

[*Aside*] How all the other passions fleet to air:
As doubtful thoughts, and rash-embrac'd despair,
And shudd'ring fear, and green-ey'd jealousy!
O love, be moderate, allay thy ecstasy,
In measure rain thy joy, scant this excess!
I feel too much thy blessing: make it less
For fear I surfeit.

Bassanio *opens the leaden casket*

Bassanio

What find I here?
Fair Portia's counterfeit! What demi-god
Hath come so near creation? Move these eyes?
Or whether riding on the balls of mine
Seem they in motion? Here are sever'd lips
Parted with sugar breath; so sweet a bar
Should sunder such sweet friends. Here in her hairs
The painter plays the spider, and hath woven
A golden mesh t'entrap the hearts of men
Faster than gnats in cobwebs. But her eyes—
How could he see to do them? Having made one,
Methinks it should have power to steal both his
And leave itself unfurnish'd. Yet look how far
The substance of my praise doth wrong this shadow
In underprizing it, so far this shadow
Doth limp behind the substance. Here's the scroll,
The continent and summary of my fortune.
[*He reads*] 'You that choose not by the view
Chance as fair, and choose as true.
Since this fortune falls to you,
Be content and seek no new.
If you be well pleas'd with this,
And hold your fortune for your bliss,
Turn to where your lady is,
And claim her with a loving kiss.'
A gentle scroll! Fair lady, by your leave,
I come by note to give, and to receive.
Like one of two contending in a prize
That thinks he hath done well in people's eyes,
Hearing applause and universal shout,
Giddy in spirit, still gazing in a doubt
Whether those peals of praise be his or no—
So, thrice-fair lady, stand I even so,
As doubtful whether what I see be true,
Until confirm'd, sign'd, ratified by you.

Portia

You see me, Lord Bassanio, where I stand,
Such as I am. Though for myself alone
I would not be ambitious in my wish

115 *counterfeit*: picture.

116 *Move . . . eyes*: do these eyes move.
117 *riding . . . mine*: fixed on my eyes.
118 *sever'd*: parted.
119 *bar*: barrier (i.e. Portia's breath).
121 *painter . . . spider*: the painter has been like a spider.
123 *Faster*: more securely.
125 *power*: i.e. like the sun; Bassanio uses a conventional conceit.
126 *unfurnish'd*: without a mate.
how far: by the extent to which.
127 *substance*: body.
shadow: semblance.
128 *underprizing it*: failing to describe it adequately.
so far: to the same extent.
130 *continent*: container.
132 *Chance . . . true*: may you have such good fortune and always choose as well.
136 *hold . . . bliss*: account your fortune happiness.
140 *by note*: with a bill of dues.
141 *prize*: match.
143 *universal*: general.

To wish myself much better, yet for you
I would be trebled twenty times myself,
A thousand times more fair, ten thousand times
More rich, that only to stand high in your account
I might in virtues, beauties, livings, friends,
Exceed account. But the full sum of me
Is sum of something: which to term in gross
Is an unlesson'd girl, unschool'd, unpractis'd;
Happy in this, she is not yet so old
But she may learn; happier than this,
She is not bred so dull but she can learn;
Happiest of all, is that her gentle spirit
Commits itself to yours to be directed
As from her lord, her governor, her king.
Myself, and what is mine, to you and yours
Is now converted. But now I was the lord
Of this fair mansion, master of my servants,
Queen o'er myself; and even now, but now,
This house, these servants, and this same myself
Are yours, my lord's. I give them with this ring,
Which when you part from, lose, or give away,
Let it presage the ruin of your love,
And be my vantage to exclaim on you.

Bassanio

Madam, you have bereft me of all words.
Only my blood speaks to you in my veins,
And there is such confusion in my powers
As after some oration fairly spoke
By a beloved prince there doth appear
Among the buzzing, pleased multitude,
Where every something being blent together
Turns to a wild of nothing, save of joy
Express'd, and not express'd. But when this ring
Parts from this finger, then parts life from hence:
O then be bold to say Bassanio's dead!

Nerissa

My lord and lady, it is now our time,
That have stood by and seen our wishes prosper,
To cry 'good joy'. Good joy, my lord and lady!

155 *That only*: only in order to.
156 *livings*: material possessions.
157 *account*: estimation.
158 *to . . . gross*: in gross terms.
159 *unpractis'd*: inexperienced.
160 *Happy*: fortunate.
162 *bred so dull*: born so stupid.
166–7 *Myself . . . converted*: I, and everything I possess, have now become your property.
167 *but now*: just a moment ago.
174 *vantage*: opportunity.
exclaim on: denounce.

175 *bereft me of*: stolen from me.
176 *my blood speaks*: Bassanio blushes.
177 *powers*: faculties.
178–83 *As . . . express'd*: Bassanio compares his mixed feelings to a happy mob of citizens after a well-delivered speech from their popular ruler.
179 *beloved*: belovèd.
180 *buzzing*: murmuring.
pleased: pleasèd.
181 *something*: little thing.
blent: blended, mixed.
182 *wild of nothing*: indistinguishable wilderness.
save: except.

190–1 *I wish . . . me*: I hope you will have all the joy you wish for yourselves, because I am sure you will not wish any of my joy away from me.

192 *solemnize*: formally celebrate.

194 *Even*: just.

195 *so*: provided that.

198 *maid*: lady-in-waiting.

199–200 *for . . . you*: I wasted no more spare time ('intermission') than you.

201 *stood*: depended.

202 *as . . . falls*: as it happens.

203 *until . . . again*: so hard that I was sweating.

204–5 *swearing . . . love*: making vows of love until the roof of my mouth was dry.

205 *if promise last*: if she keeps the promise; Gratiano puns on two senses of a word (also in line 211).

206 *of*: from.

209 *so . . . withal*: provided that you are pleased with it.

210 *mean good faith*: have good intentions.

211 *'faith*: upon my faith.

213–14 *We'll . . . ducats*: we'll wager a thousand ducats on who has the first son.

215 *stake down*: money for the bet laid on the table; Gratiano takes the slang sense 'with a limp penis'.

216 *infidel*: Gratiano refers to Jessica's Jewishness.

Gratiano

My lord Bassanio, and my gentle lady,
I wish you all the joy that you can wish;
For I am sure you can wish none from me.
And when your honours mean to solemnize
The bargain of your faith, I do beseech you
Even at that time I may be married too.

Bassanio

With all my heart, so thou canst get a wife.

Gratiano

I thank your lordship, you have got me one.
My eyes, my lord, can look as swift as yours:
You saw the mistress, I beheld the maid.
You lov'd, I lov'd; for intermission
No more pertains to me, my lord, than you.
Your fortune stood upon the caskets there,
And so did mine too as the matter falls.
For wooing here until I sweat again,
And swearing till my very roof was dry
With oaths of love, at last—if promise last—
I got a promise of this fair one here
To have her love, provided that your fortune
Achiev'd her mistress.

Portia

Is this true, Nerissa?

Nerissa

Madam, it is, so you stand pleas'd withal.

Bassanio

And do you, Gratiano, mean good faith?

Gratiano

Yes 'faith, my lord.

Bassanio

Our feast shall be much honour'd in your marriage.

Gratiano

We'll play with them the first boy for a thousand ducats.

Nerissa

What, and stake down?

Gratiano

No, we shall ne'er win at that sport and stake down.
But who comes here? Lorenzo and his infidel!
What, and my old Venetian friend Salerio!

Enter Lorenzo, Jessica, *and* Salerio, *a messenger from Venice*

Bassanio

Lorenzo and Salerio, welcome hither—
If that the youth of my new interest here
Have power to bid you welcome. By your leave
I bid my very friends and countrymen,
Sweet Portia, welcome.

Portia

So do I, my lord.
They are entirely welcome.

Lorenzo

I thank your honour. For my part, my lord,
My purpose was not to have seen you here,
But meeting with Salerio by the way
He did entreat me past all saying nay
To come with him along.

Salerio

I did, my lord,
And I have reason for it. [*Giving letter*] Signor Antonio
Commends him to you.

Bassanio

Ere I ope his letter,
I pray you tell me how my good friend doth.

Salerio

Not sick, my lord, unless it be in mind,
Nor well, unless in mind: his letter there
Will show you his estate.

Bassanio *opens the letter*

Gratiano

Nerissa, cheer yond stranger, bid her welcome.
Your hand, Salerio; what's the news from Venice?
How doth that royal merchant, good Antonio?
I know he will be glad of our success;
We are the Jasons, we have won the fleece.

Salerio

I would you had won the fleece that he hath lost.

219–20 *If . . . welcome*: if my very new position here gives me the right to welcome you.
221 *very*: true.
223 *entirely*: heartily.
225 *My purpose was not*: I did not intend.
226 *by the way*: by chance.
227 *past . . . nay*: and would not let me refuse.
230 *Commends him*: sends his greetings.
233 *in mind*: in fortitude.
234 *estate*: condition.
235 *cheer*: welcome.
yond: yonder.
237 *royal*: prince among merchants.
239 *Jasons*: See note on *1*, 1, 170.
240 *fleece*: Salerio puns on 'fleets'.

Portia

There are some shrewd contents in yond same paper
That steals the colour from Bassanio's cheek:
Some dear friend dead, else nothing in the world
Could turn so much the constitution
Of any constant man. What, worse and worse?
With leave, Bassanio, I am half yourself
And I must freely have the half of anything
That this same paper brings you.

Bassanio

O sweet Portia,
Here are a few of the unpleasant'st words
That ever blotted paper. Gentle lady,
When I did first impart my love to you,
I freely told you all the wealth I had
Ran in my veins: I was a gentleman.
And then I told you true; and yet, dear lady,
Rating myself at nothing, you shall see
How much I was a braggart. When I told you
My state was nothing, I should then have told you
That I was worse than nothing; for indeed
I have engag'd myself to a dear friend,
Engag'd my friend to his mere enemy,
To feed my means. Here is a letter, lady,
The paper as the body of my friend,
And every word in it a gaping wound
Issuing lifeblood. But is it true, Salerio?
Hath all his ventures failed? What, not one hit?
From Tripolis, from Mexico, and England,
From Lisbon, Barbary, and India,
And not one vessel 'scape the dreadful touch
Of merchant-marring rocks?

Salerio

Not one, my lord.
Besides, it should appear that if he had
The present money to discharge the Jew,
He would not take it. Never did I know
A creature that did bear the shape of man
So keen and greedy to confound a man.
He plies the duke at morning and at night,

241 *shrewd*: bitter.

244 *constitution*: complexion.

245 *constant*: normal.

246 *With leave*: excuse me.

250 *blotted paper*: spoiled a paper with ink.

252 *freely*: honestly.

253 *Ran in my veins*: was in my blood.

255 *Rating*: valuing.

256 *was a braggart*: boasted.

259 *engag'd*: bound.

260 *mere*: absolute.

261 *To feed my means*: to get the money I needed.

262 *as*: is like.

264 *Issuing lifeblood*: from which his lifeblood pours.

265 *ventures*: speculations.
hit: succeeded.

269 *merchant-marring rocks*: rocks that ruin merchants.

271 *present*: ready.
discharge: pay his debt to.

275 *plies*: urges his case on.

276 *impeach . . . state*: discredit the integrity of Venetian law.

278 *magnificoes*: noblemen.

279 *port*: eminence.
persuaded: argued.

280 *drive him from*: persuade him to give up.
envious plea: malicious claim.

283 *his countrymen*: fellow Jews.

287 *deny not*: do not prevent it.

288 *hard*: badly.

291 *best condition'd*: most good-natured.

292 *courtesies*: acts of kindness.

293 *The ancient Roman honour*: i.e. loyalty to friends and country.

297 *deface*: cancel.

301 *call me wife*: make me your wife.

309 *shall hence*: must go away from here.

And doth impeach the freedom of the state
If they deny him justice. Twenty merchants,
The duke himself, and the magnificoes
Of greatest port have all persuaded with him,
But none can drive him from the envious plea
Of forfeiture, of justice, and his bond.

Jessica

When I was with him, I have heard him swear
To Tubal and to Chus, his countrymen,
That he would rather have Antonio's flesh
Than twenty times the value of the sum
That he did owe him; and I know, my lord,
If law, authority, and power deny not
It will go hard with poor Antonio.

Portia

Is it your dear friend that is thus in trouble?

Bassanio

The dearest friend to me, the kindest man,
The best condition'd and unwearied spirit
In doing courtesies; and one in whom
The ancient Roman honour more appears
Than any that draws breath in Italy.

Portia

What sums owes he the Jew?

Bassanio

For me, three thousand ducats.

Portia

What, no more?
Pay him six thousand, and deface the bond.
Double six thousand, and then treble that,
Before a friend of this description
Shall lose a hair through Bassanio's fault.
First go with me to church, and call me wife,
And then away to Venice to your friend!
For never shall you lie by Portia's side
With an unquiet soul. You shall have gold
To pay the petty debt twenty times over.
When it is paid, bring your true friend along.
My maid Nerissa and myself meantime
Will live as maids and widows. Come away,
For you shall hence upon your wedding day.

310 *cheer*: face.
311 *dear bought*: expensively purchased.
313 *miscarried*: been lost.
316 *cleared*: cancelled.
317 *but*: only.
318 *use your pleasure*: do as you please.
320 *Dispatch*: quickly finish.
321 *good leave*: kind permission.
323–4 *No . . . twain*: no bed will be accused of holding me back, and no rest shall come between the two of us.

Bid your friends welcome, show a merry cheer;
Since you are dear bought, I will love you dear.
But let me hear the letter of your friend.

Bassanio

[*Reads*] 'Sweet Bassanio, my ships have all miscarried, my creditors grow cruel, my estate is very low; my bond to the Jew is forfeit, and since in paying it, it is impossible I should live, all debts are cleared between you and I if I might but see you at my death. Notwithstanding, use your pleasure; if your love do not persuade you to come, let not my letter.'

Portia

O love! Dispatch all business and be gone.

Bassanio

Since I have your good leave to go away,
I will make haste. But till I come again
No bed shall e'er be guilty of my stay
Nor rest be interposer 'twixt us twain. [*Exeunt*

Act 3 Scene 3
Antonio has been arrested and Shylock threatens him.

Scene 3

Venice: a street. Enter Shylock *the Jew, and* Solanio, *and* Antonio, *and the* Jailer

1 *look to him*: guard him carefully.
2 *gratis*: free of interest.
4 *speak not*: don't argue.
5 *my bond*: Shylock emphasizes the legality of his claim.

Shylock

Jailer, look to him. Tell not me of mercy.
This is the fool that lent out money gratis.
Jailer, look to him.

Antonio

Hear me yet, good Shylock—

Shylock

I'll have my bond, speak not against my bond;
I have sworn an oath that I will have my bond.

8–10 *I . . . request*: It would appear that Antonio is being given some unusual privileges.
9 *naughty*: worthless.
fond: foolish.
10 *abroad*: out of the prison.

14 *dull-eyed*: stupid.
16 *intercessors*: pleaders.
18 *impenetrable*: hard-hearted.
19 *kept with*: lived among.
20 *bootless*: unsuccessful.

22 *deliver'd*: rescued.
forfeitures: actions for breach of contract (like that which Antonio now endures).
23 *made moan*: complained.

25 *grant*: allow.

27 *commodity*: privilege.
strangers: foreigners.

29 *impeach*: discredit.

31 *Consisteth of*: depends upon.
32 *bated me*: made me lose weight.

34 *bloody*: bloodthirsty.

Thou call'dst me dog before thou hadst a cause,
But since I am a dog, beware my fangs.
The duke shall grant me justice. I do wonder,
Thou naughty jailer, that thou art so fond
To come abroad with him at his request.

Antonio
I pray thee hear me speak—

Shylock
I'll have my bond; I will not hear thee speak;
I'll have my bond, and therefore speak no more.
I'll not be made a soft and dull-eyed fool,
To shake the head, relent, and sigh, and yield
To Christian intercessors. Follow not!
I'll have no speaking, I will have my bond. [*Exit*

Solanio
It is the most impenetrable cur
That ever kept with men.

Antonio
Let him alone.
I'll follow him no more with bootless prayers.
He seeks my life, his reason well I know:
I oft deliver'd from his forfeitures
Many that have at times made moan to me;
Therefore he hates me.

Solanio
I am sure the duke
Will never grant this forfeiture to hold.

Antonio
The duke cannot deny the course of law;
For the commodity that strangers have
With us in Venice, if it be denied,
Will much impeach the justice of the state,
Since that the trade and profit of the city
Consisteth of all nations. Therefore go.
These griefs and losses have so bated me
That I shall hardly spare a pound of flesh
Tomorrow to my bloody creditor.
Well, jailer, on. Pray God Bassanio come
To see me pay his debt, and then I care not. [*Exeunt*

Act 3 Scene 4
Portia and Nerissa plan a visit to Venice.

Scene 4

Belmont: Portia*'s house. Enter* Portia, Nerissa, Lorenzo, Jessica, *and* Balthazar *a man of* Portia*'s*

Lorenzo
Madam, although I speak it in your presence,
You have a noble and a true conceit
Of god-like amity, which appears most strongly
In bearing thus the absence of your lord.
But if you knew to whom you show this honour,
How true a gentleman you send relief,
How dear a lover of my lord your husband,
I know you would be prouder of the work
Than customary bounty can enforce you.

Portia
I never did repent for doing good,
Nor shall not now; for in companions
That do converse and waste the time together,
Whose souls do bear an equal yoke of love,
There must be needs a like proportion
Of lineaments, of manners, and of spirit;
Which makes me think that this Antonio,
Being the bosom lover of my lord,
Must needs be like my lord. If it be so,
How little is the cost I have bestow'd
In purchasing the semblance of my soul
From out the state of hellish cruelty!
This comes too near the praising of myself,
Therefore no more of it: hear other things.
Lorenzo, I commit into your hands
The husbandry and manage of my house
Until my lord's return; for mine own part
I have toward heaven breath'd a secret vow
To live in prayer and contemplation,
Only attended by Nerissa here,
Until her husband and my lord's return.
There is a monastery two miles off,
And there we will abide. I do desire you
Not to deny this imposition,

2 *conceit*: understanding.
3 *amity*: friendship.
5 *to whom*: i.e. Antonio.
7 *lover*: friend.
9 *customary . . . you*: your usual generosity must make you feel.
12 *waste*: spend.
13 *bear . . . love*: are joined equally together in love.
14 *needs*: of necessity.
like: similar.
15 *lineaments*: appearances.
17 *bosom lover*: intimate friend.
19 *bestow'd*: spent.
20 *semblance . . . soul*: likeness of the one I love.
22 *comes too near*: is too like.
25 *husbandry and manage*: careful management.
33 *deny*: refuse.
imposition: task.

The which my love and some necessity
Now lays upon you.

Lorenzo

Madam, with all my heart
I shall obey you in all fair commands.

Portia

My people do already know my mind,
And will acknowledge you and Jessica
In place of Lord Bassanio and myself.
So fare you well till we shall meet again.

Lorenzo

Fair thoughts and happy hours attend on you.

Jessica

I wish your ladyship all heart's content.

Portia

I thank you for your wish, and am well pleas'd
To wish it back on you: fare you well, Jessica.
[*Exeunt* Jessica *and* Lorenzo
Now, Balthazar—
As I have ever found thee honest-true,
So let me find thee still; take this same letter,
And use thou all th'endeavour of a man
In speed to Padua. See thou render this
Into my cousin's hand, Doctor Bellario;
And look, what notes and garments he doth give thee
Bring them, I pray thee, with imagin'd speed
Unto the traject, to the common ferry
Which trades to Venice. Waste no time in words
But get thee gone; I shall be there before thee.

Balthazar

Madam, I go with all convenient speed. [*Exit*

Portia

Come on, Nerissa; I have work in hand
That you yet know not of. We'll see our husbands
Before they think of us.

Nerissa

Shall they see us?

Portia

They shall, Nerissa, but in such a habit
That they shall think we are accomplished

37 *people*: household.
my mind: what I intend.
38 *acknowledge*: recognize your authority.
44 *wish . . . you*: with the same to you.
45 *Now, Balthazar*: The broken line allows for movement on the stage.
46 *ever*: always.
honest-true: honest and trustworthy.
47 *So . . . still*: may I continue to find you so.
48 *all . . . man*: go as fast as a man can.
49 *render*: give.
51 *what*: whatever.
52 *imagin'd speed*: all the speed imaginable.
53 *the traject . . . ferry*: the ferry, the public transport.
54 *trades to*: communicates with.
56 *convenient*: appropriate.
57 *work in hand*: a plan in my mind.
59 *think of us*: expect to see us.
60 *habit*: costume.
61 *accomplished*: accomplishèd; equipped.

With that we lack. I'll hold thee any wager,
When we are both accoutred like young men
I'll prove the prettier fellow of the two,
And wear my dagger with the braver grace,
And speak between the change of man and boy
With a reed voice, and turn two mincing steps
Into a manly stride; and speak of 'frays
Like a fine bragging youth; and tell quaint lies
How honourable ladies sought my love,
Which I denying, they fell sick and died—
I could not do withal. Then I'll repent,
And wish for all that that I had not kill'd them;
And twenty of these puny lies I'll tell,
That men shall swear I have discontinu'd school
Above a twelvemonth. I have within my mind
A thousand raw tricks of these bragging jacks,
Which I will practise.

Nerissa

Why, shall we turn to men?

Portia

Fie, what a question's that,
If thou wert near a lewd interpreter!
But come, I'll tell thee all my whole device
When I am in my coach, which stays for us
At the park gate; and therefore haste away,
For we must measure twenty miles today. [*Exeunt*

62 *that we lack*: i.e. male genitals.
63 *accoutred*: dressed up.
64 *prettier*: smarter.
66 *between . . . boy*: as though my voice were breaking.
67 *reed*: squeaky.
mincing: dainty, ladylike.
68 *'frays*: affrays, fights.
69 *bragging*: boastful.
quaint: elaborate.
72 *do withal*: help it.
75–6 *I have . . . twelvemonth*: it's more than a year since I left school (i.e. I'm a real man).
77 *raw*: crude.
jacks: fellows.
78 *turn to men*: change into men. Portia pretends to think that Nerissa means 'take men for lovers'.
80 *lewd interpreter*: someone with a dirty mind.
81 *device*: plan.
84 *measure*: travel.

Scene 5

Act 3 Scene 5
Lancelot teases Jessica.

Belmont: Portia*'s garden. Enter* Lancelot *the Clown and* Jessica

Lancelot

Yes truly, for look you, the sins of the father are to be laid upon the children. Therefore I promise you I fear you. I was always plain with you, and so now I speak my agitation of the matter. Therefore be o'good cheer, for truly I think you are damned. There is but one hope in it that can do you any good, and that is but a kind of bastard hope neither.

1 *look you*: you see.
1–2 *the sins . . . children*: Lancelot quotes from the Second Commandment (Exodus 20:5).
2 *laid upon*: revenged upon.
2–3 *I fear you*: I fear for you.
3 *plain*: honest.
4 *agitation*: Lancelot means 'cogitation' (= considered opinion).
7 *bastard hope*: a) false hope; b) hope that you are a bastard.
neither: anyway.

Jessica

And what hope is that, I pray thee?

Lancelot

Marry, you may partly hope that your father got you not, that you are not the Jew's daughter.

Jessica

That were a kind of bastard hope indeed; so the sins of my mother should be visited upon me.

Lancelot

Truly, then, I fear you are damned both by father and mother; thus when I shun Scylla your father, I fall into Charybdis your mother. Well, you are gone both ways.

Jessica

I shall be saved by my husband; he hath made me a Christian.

Lancelot

Truly, the more to blame he; we were Christians enow before, e'en as many as could well live one by another. This making of Christians will raise the price of hogs; if we grow all to be pork eaters, we shall not shortly have a rasher on the coals for money.

Enter Lorenzo

Jessica

I'll tell my husband, Lancelot, what you say: here he comes.

Lorenzo

I shall grow jealous of you shortly, Lancelot, if you thus get my wife into corners.

Jessica

Nay, you need not fear us, Lorenzo: Lancelot and I are out. He tells me flatly there's no mercy for me in heaven, because I am a Jew's daughter; and he says you are no good member of the commonwealth, for in converting Jews to Christians you raise the price of pork.

Lorenzo

I shall answer that better to the commonwealth than you can the getting up of the Negro's belly: the Moor is with child by you, Lancelot.

9 *got*: begot, fathered.

11 *so*: if that were the case.

12 *visited*: revenged.

14–15 *Scylla . . . Charybdis*: Monsters (a rock-formation and a whirlpool) threatening sailors of classical mythology in the narrow straits between Italy and Sicily.

15 *gone*: ruined, damned.

16 *saved . . . husband*: Jessica can quote St Paul: 'the unbelieving wife is sanctified by the husband' (1 Corinthians 7:14).

18 *enow*: enough.

19 *e'en . . . another*: just enough to live comfortably together.

21 *pork eaters*: Jews are forbidden to eat pork.

21–2 *not . . . money*: soon not be able to afford a rasher of fried bacon.

27–8 *are out*: have quarrelled.

30 *commonwealth*: general public.

33 *getting up*: swelling out.
Moor: Moorish woman (probably a servant).

Lancelot

It is much that the Moor should be more than reason; but if she be less than an honest woman, she is indeed more than I took her for.

Lorenzo

How every fool can play upon the word! I think the best grace of wit will shortly turn into silence, and discourse grow commendable in none only but parrots. Go in, sirrah, bid them prepare for dinner.

Lancelot

That is done, sir; they have all stomachs.

Lorenzo

Goodly Lord, what a witsnapper are you! Then bid them prepare dinner.

Lancelot

That is done too, sir; only 'cover' is the word.

Lorenzo

Will you cover then, sir?

Lancelot

Not so, sir, neither; I know my duty.

Lorenzo

Yet more quarrelling with occasion! Wilt thou show the whole wealth of thy wit in an instant? I pray thee understand a plain man in his plain meaning: go to thy fellows, bid them cover the table, serve in the meat, and we will come in to dinner.

Lancelot

For the table, sir, it shall be served in; for the meat, sir, it shall be covered; for your coming in to dinner, sir, why, let it be as humours and conceits shall govern. [*Exit*

Lorenzo

O dear discretion, how his words are suited!
The fool hath planted in his memory
An army of good words; and I do know
A many fools that stand in better place,
Garnish'd like him, that for a tricksy word
Defy the matter. How cheer'st thou, Jessica?
And now, good sweet, say thy opinion:
How dost thou like the Lord Bassanio's wife?

35 *more than reason*: bigger than she ought to be; Lancelot cannot resist a pun.

36–7 *if . . . for*: if she's not an honest (= chaste) woman, she's certainly more than I thought she was.

38–40 *the best . . . parrots*: silence will soon be the finest display of intelligence, and only parrots will be praised for conversation.

42 *have all stomachs*: are all hungry.

43 *witsnapper*: punster, comedian.

45 *'cover' . . . word*: you should say 'cover' (meaning a) prepare the table; b) put on your hat).

47 *duty*: place, respect; servants stood bare-headed in the presence of superiors.

48 *quarrelling with occasion*: taking every opportunity for quibbles.

55 *as . . . govern*: as your whims and fancies take you.

56 *discretion*: sagacity, judgement.
suited: matched.

59 *A many fools*: a lot of professional jesters.
stand . . . place: have higher positions.

60 *Garnish'd*: trimmed up; Lorenzo refers to the extra braid on Lancelot's livery (see *2*, 2, 144) which makes him look like a jester.
tricksy: clever, playful.

61 *Defy the matter*: contradict the sense.
How . . . thou: how are you getting on.

Jessica

Past all expressing. It is very meet
The Lord Bassanio live an upright life,
For having such a blessing in his lady
He finds the joys of heaven here on earth,
And if on earth he do not merit it,
In reason he should never come to heaven.
Why, if two gods should play some heavenly match,
And on the wager lay two earthly women,
And Portia one, there must be something else
Pawn'd with the other, for the poor rude world
Hath not her fellow.

Lorenzo

Even such a husband
Hast thou of me, as she is for a wife.

Jessica

Nay, but ask my opinion too of that.

Lorenzo

I will anon; first let us go to dinner.

Jessica

Nay, let me praise you while I have a stomach.

Lorenzo

No, pray thee, let it serve for table talk;
Then howsome'er thou speak'st, 'mong other things
I shall digest it.

Jessica

Well, I'll set you forth. [*Exeunt*

64 *Past all expressing*: beyond words.
meet: proper, right.
65 *upright*: virtuous.
73 *Pawn'd*: gambled.
74 *fellow*: equal, match.
77 *anon*: shortly.
78 *stomach*: a) appetite; b) inclination.
79 *table talk*: mealtime conversation.
80 *howsome'er*: however.
81 *set you forth*: put you in your place.

Act 4

Act 4 Scene 1
Antonio is prepared to die when Shylock refuses to show mercy, but Portia, disguised as a young lawyer, tricks Shylock out of his bond. Then she asks Bassanio for his ring as a reward.

Scene 1

Venice: the courtroom. Enter the Duke, *the* Magnificoes, Antonio, Bassanio, Salerio, *and* Gratiano *with others.*

Duke
What, is Antonio here?

Antonio
Ready, so please your grace.

Duke
I am sorry for thee. Thou art come to answer
A stony adversary, an inhuman wretch,
Uncapable of pity, void and empty
From any dram of mercy.

Antonio
I have heard
Your grace hath tane great pains to qualify
His rigorous course; but since he stands obdurate
And that no lawful means can carry me
Out of his envy's reach, I do oppose
My patience to his fury, and am arm'd
To suffer with a quietness of spirit
The very tyranny and rage of his.

Duke
Go one and call the Jew into the court.

Salerio
He is ready at the door; he comes, my lord.

Enter Shylock

Duke
Make room and let him stand before our face.
Shylock, the world thinks, and I think so too,
That thou but leadest this fashion of thy malice
To the last hour of act, and then 'tis thought

2 *Ready*: present.

3 *answer*: defend yourself against.

5 *void*: barren.

6 *From*: of.
dram: a tiny measure.

7 *qualify*: moderate.

8 *obdurate*: obdùrate; firm, resolute.

10 *envy*: malice.

13 *The . . . his*: all the cruel power and anger of his spirit.

18–19 *thou . . . act*: you intend to carry on with this show of cruelty until the very last moment.

20 *remorse*: pity.
more strange: even more unusual.
21 *strange apparent*: apparently abnormal.
22 *exacts*: demand.
24 *loose the forfeiture*: surrender the forfeit (i.e. the pound of flesh).
26 *Forgive . . . principal*: forgo a certain amount of the sum he borrowed.
29 *Enow*: enough.
royal merchant: even such a substantial merchant prince.
30 *commiseration of*: sympathy for.
31 *brassy bosoms*: hearts as hard as brass.
32 *stubborn*: unfeeling.
32–3 *train'd . . . courtesy*: taught to behave with gentleness.
35 *possess'd*: informed.
36 *Sabaoth*: In Hebrew this word means 'armies'; many editions read 'Sabbath' (= Saturday, the holiest day of the Jewish week).
37 *due and forfeit*: forfeit which is due.
38 *light*: alight, descend.
39 *charter . . . freedom*: city's independence granted by charter.
41 *carrion*: rotten.
43 *humour*: whimsy, fancy.
is it answer'd: will that do for an answer.
46 *ban'd*: poisoned.
47 *gaping pig*: roasted pig's head (with an apple in its mouth).
49 *sings i'the nose*: drones.
50–1 *affection . . . passion*: instinctive (physical) reaction often overcomes emotion (see *3*, 1, 53).
54–6 *he*: this man . . . that man . . . another man.
56 *woollen*: The leather bag of the bagpipes was covered with sheepskin.
of force: involuntarily.

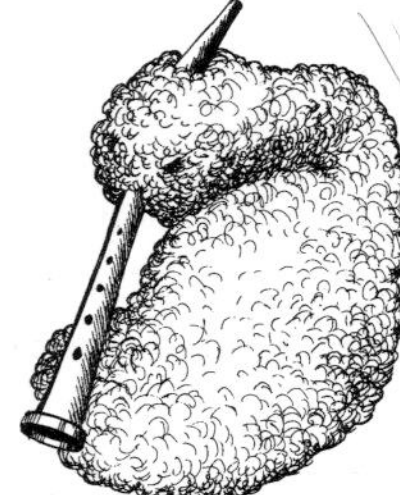

57 *shame*: embarrassment.
58 *to offend*: give offence to others.

Thou'lt show thy mercy and remorse more strange
Than is thy strange apparent cruelty.
And where thou now exacts the penalty,
Which is a pound of this poor merchant's flesh,
Thou wilt not only loose the forfeiture
But, touch'd with human gentleness and love,
Forgive a moiety of the principal,
Glancing an eye of pity on his losses
That have of late so huddl'd on his back,
Enow to press a royal merchant down
And pluck commiseration of his state
From brassy bosoms and rough hearts of flint,
From stubborn Turks, and Tartars never train'd
To offices of tender courtesy.
We all expect a gentle answer, Jew.

Shylock

I have possess'd your grace of what I purpose,
And by our holy Sabaoth have I sworn
To have the due and forfeit of my bond.
If you deny it, let the danger light
Upon your charter and your city's freedom!
You'll ask me why I rather choose to have
A weight of carrion flesh than to receive
Three thousand ducats. I'll not answer that—
But say it is my humour: is it answer'd?
What if my house be troubled with a rat,
And I be pleas'd to give ten thousand ducats
To have it ban'd? What, are you answer'd yet?
Some men there are love not a gaping pig;
Some that are mad if they behold a cat;
And others when the bagpipe sings i'the nose
Cannot contain their urine: for affection
Masters oft passion, sways it to the mood
Of what it likes or loathes. Now for your answer:
As there is no firm reason to be render'd
Why he cannot abide a gaping pig,
Why he a harmless necessary cat,
Why he a woollen bagpipe, but of force
Must yield to such inevitable shame
As to offend, himself being offended:
So can I give no reason, nor I will not,

60 *lodg'd*: deep-rooted.
certain: steadfast.

62 *losing*: unprofitable.

64 *current*: outpouring.

68 *offence*: displeasure.

70 *think . . . Jew*: remember that you are arguing with the Jew.

72 *main flood*: ocean tide.
bate: reduce.

73 *use question with*: ask.

77 *fretten*: blown.

82 *with . . . conveniency*: as quickly and simply as possible.

87 *draw*: take.

More than a lodg'd hate and a certain loathing
I bear Antonio, that I follow thus
A losing suit against him. Are you answer'd?

Bassanio

This is no answer, thou unfeeling man,
To excuse the current of thy cruelty.

Shylock

I am not bound to please thee with my answers.

Bassanio

Do all men kill the things they do not love?

Shylock

Hates any man the thing he would not kill?

Bassanio

Every offence is not a hate at first.

Shylock

What, wouldst thou have a serpent sting thee twice?

Antonio

I pray you think you question with the Jew.
You may as well go stand upon the beach
And bid the main flood bate his usual height;
You may as well use question with the wolf
Why he hath made the ewe bleat for the lamb;
You may as well forbid the mountain pines
To wag their high tops and to make no noise
When they are fretten with the gusts of heaven;
You may as well do anything most hard
As seek to soften that—than which what's harder?—
His Jewish heart. Therefore I do beseech you
Make no moe offers, use no farther means,
But with all brief and plain conveniency
Let me have judgement, and the Jew his will.

Bassanio

For thy three thousand ducats here is six.

Shylock

If every ducat in six thousand ducats
Were in six parts, and every part a ducat,
I would not draw them; I would have my bond.

Duke

How shalt thou hope for mercy, rendering none?

Shylock

What judgement shall I dread, doing no wrong?

90 *purchas'd slave*: slave that you have bought.

92 *parts*: tasks, duties.

97 *Be season'd . . . viands*: be treated with the same food as your own.

101 *fie*: shame.

102 *force*: power.

104 *Upon my power*: with my authority.

106 *determine this*: resolve this dispute.

107 *stays without*: is waiting outside.

114 *tainted*: sick, contaminated.
wether: castrated ram.

115 *Meetest*: most suitable.

118 *live still*: go on living.

You have among you many a purchas'd slave,
Which, like your asses and your dogs and mules,
You use in abject and in slavish parts
Because you bought them. Shall I say to you,
'Let them be free! Marry them to your heirs!
Why sweat they under burdens? Let their beds
Be made as soft as yours, and let their palates
Be season'd with such viands'? You will answer,
'The slaves are ours.' So do I answer you.
The pound of flesh which I demand of him
Is dearly bought; 'tis mine, and I will have it.
If you deny me, fie upon your law:
There is no force in the decrees of Venice.
I stand for judgement. Answer: shall I have it?

Duke

Upon my power I may dismiss this court,
Unless Bellario, a learned doctor
Whom I have sent for to determine this,
Come here today.

Salerio

My lord, here stays without
A messenger with letters from the doctor,
New come from Padua.

Duke

Bring us the letters. Call the messenger.

Bassanio

Good cheer, Antonio! What, man, courage yet!
The Jew shall have my flesh, blood, bones and all,
Ere thou shalt lose for me one drop of blood.

Antonio

I am a tainted wether of the flock,
Meetest for death; the weakest kind of fruit
Drops earliest to the ground, and so let me.
You cannot better be employ'd, Bassanio,
Than to live still and write mine epitaph.

Enter Nerissa *disguised as a lawyer's clerk*

Duke

Came you from Padua, from Bellario?

Nerissa
From both, my lord: [*Presenting letter*] Bellario greets your grace.
Bassanio
Why dost thou whet thy knife so earnestly?
Shylock
To cut the forfeiture from that bankrupt there.
Gratiano
Not on thy sole, but on thy soul, harsh Jew,
Thou mak'st thy knife keen. But no metal can,
No, not the hangman's axe, bear half the keenness
Of thy sharp envy. Can no prayers pierce thee?
Shylock
No, none that thou hast wit enough to make.
Gratiano
O be thou damn'd, inexecrable dog,
And for thy life let justice be accus'd!
Thou almost mak'st me waver in my faith,
To hold opinion with Pythagoras
That souls of animals infuse themselves
Into the trunks of men. Thy currish spirit
Govern'd a wolf, who—hang'd for human slaughter—
Even from the gallows did his fell soul fleet,
And whilst thou layest in thy unhallow'd dam
Infus'd itself in thee; for thy desires
Are wolfish, bloody, starv'd, and ravenous.
Shylock
Till thou canst rail the seal from off my bond
Thou but offend'st thy lungs to speak so loud.
Repair thy wit, good youth, or it will fall
To cureless ruin. I stand here for law.
Duke
This letter from Bellario doth commend
A young and learned doctor to our court:
Where is he?
Nerissa
He attendeth here hard by
To know your answer whether you'll admit him.

121 *whet*: sharpen.
123 *thy sole*: the sole of your shoe.
125 *hangman*: executioner.
127 *wit*: sense, intelligence.
128 *inexecrable*: unspeakably damned.
129 *for . . . accus'd*: only a failure of justice allows you to live.
131 *hold opinion*: agree.
Pythagoras: a Greek philosopher who believed in the transmigration of souls—explained here by Gratiano.
132 *infuse*: pour.
133 *currish*: like a cur—a mongrel dog.
134 *hang'd . . . slaughter*: executed as a murderer.
135 *Even . . . fleet*: let his cruel soul pass straight from the gallows.
136 *unhallow'd dam*: unholy (non-Christian) mother.
139 *rail*: shout.
140 *but offend'st*: are only hurting.
142 *cureless*: incurable.
145 *hard*: near.

Duke

With all my heart. Some three of four of you
Go give him courteous conduct to this place.

[*Exeunt* officials

Meantime the court shall hear Bellario's letter.

[*Reads*] 'Your grace shall understand, that at the receipt of your letter I am very sick; but in the instant that your messenger came, in loving visitation was with me a young doctor of Rome: his name is Balthazar. I acquainted him with the cause in controversy between the Jew and Antonio the merchant. We turned o'er many books together; he is furnished with my opinion which, bettered with his own learning, the greatness whereof I cannot enough commend, comes with him at my importunity, to fill up your grace's request in my stead. I beseech you let his lack of years be no impediment to let him lack a reverend estimation, for I never knew so young a body with so old a head. I leave him to your gracious acceptance, whose trial shall better publish his commendation.'

Enter Portia *disguised as* Doctor Balthazar, *followed by* officials

You hear the learn'd Bellario what he writes,
And here I take it is the doctor come.
Give me your hand. Come you from old Bellario?

Portia

I did, my lord.

Duke

You are welcome; take your place.
Are you acquainted with the difference
That holds this present question in the court?

Portia

I am informed throughly of the cause.
Which is the merchant here and which the Jew?

Duke

Antonio and old Shylock, both stand forth.

Portia

Is your name Shylock?

148 *give . . . conduct*: escort him courteously.

152 *in loving visitation*: on a friendly visit.

154 *cause*: matter.
controversy: dispute.

155 *turned o'er*: looked through.

156 *is furnished*: has been given.

157 *bettered*: improved.

159 *importunity*: earnest request.

160–1 *let . . . estimation*: do not think poorly of him because he is young.

163–4 *whose . . . commendation*: giving him a trial will show you how much better he is than my praise.

169–70 *the difference . . . court*: the dispute that is at present on trial in this court.

171 *informed*: informèd.
throughly: thoroughly.

Shylock

Shylock is my name.

Portia

Of a strange nature is the suit you follow,
Yet in such rule that the Venetian law
Cannot impugn you as you do proceed.
—You stand within his danger, do you not?

Antonio

Ay, so he says.

Portia

Do you confess the bond?

Antonio

I do.

Portia

Then must the Jew be merciful.

Shylock

On what compulsion must I? Tell me that.

Portia

The quality of mercy is not strain'd,
It droppeth as the gentle rain from heaven
Upon the place beneath. It is twice blest:
It blesseth him that gives, and him that takes.
'Tis mightiest in the mightiest, it becomes
The throned monarch better than his crown.
His sceptre shows the force of temporal power,
The attribute to awe and majesty,
Wherein doth sit the dread and fear of kings;
But mercy is above this sceptred sway.
It is enthroned in the hearts of kings,
It is an attribute to God himself,
And early power doth then show likest God's
When mercy seasons justice. Therefore, Jew,
Though justice be thy plea, consider this:
That in the course of justice, none of us
Should see salvation. We do pray for mercy,
And that same prayer doth teach us all to render
The deeds of mercy. I have spoke thus much
To mitigate the justice of thy plea,
Which if thou follow, this strict court of Venice
Must needs give sentence 'gainst the merchant there.

176 *in such rule*: so correctly.
177 *impugn*: oppose.
178 *within his danger*: at his mercy.
180 *must*: is morally obliged to.
181 *must I*: am I forced to.
182 *is not strain'd*: cannot be constrained (= forced).
186 *mightiest . . . mightiest*: the most powerful weapon possessed by the most powerful person.
becomes: suits, is appropriate for.
187 *throned*: thronèd.
188 *temporal*: earthly.
189 *attribute*: proper possession.
190 *Wherein . . . kings*: in which (symbolically) resides the power of kings to command dread and fear.
191 *this sceptred sway*: the world ruled by kings.
192 *enthroned*: enthronèd.
193 *attribute to*: quality belonging to.
195 *seasons*: moderates.
195–200 *Therefore . . . mercy*: Portia reminds Christians of the petition of the Lord's Prayer ('Forgive us our trespasses as we forgive them that trespass against us'), and Shylock should remember Psalm 143:2 ('Enter not into judgement with thy servants: for in thy sight shall no man living be justified').
201 *mitigate . . . plea*: moderate your plea for strict justice.
203 *needs*: of necessity.

‘I crave the law, The penalty and forfeit of my bond.’ (*4*, 1, 204–5). Prunella Scales as Portia and Timothy West as Shylock, Old Vic Theatre, 1981.

204 *My . . . head*: I will be responsible for what I am doing.
crave: beg.

206 *discharge*: repay.

207 *tender*: offer.

212 *bears down*: overcomes.

213 *Wrest*: twist.
once: on this one occasion.
to: with.

215 *curb*: restrain.

217 *established*: establishèd.

221 *Daniel*: The story of Susannah and the Elders in the Apocrypha tells how a young man, sent to give judgement when Susannah was accused of unchastity, turned the evidence of the old men against themselves.

225 *thrice*: Portia seems to be raising the offer of line 208.

Shylock
My deeds upon my head! I crave the law,
The penalty and forfeit of my bond.

Portia
Is he not able to discharge the money?

Bassanio
Yes, here I tender it for him in the court,
Yea, twice the sum; if that will not suffice,
I will be bound to pay it ten times o'er
On forfeit of my hands, my head, my heart.
If this will not suffice, it must appear
That malice bears down truth. And I beseech you
Wrest once the law to your authority;
To do a great right, do a little wrong,
And curb this cruel devil of his will.

Portia
It must not be; there is no power in Venice
Can alter a decree established.
'Twill be recorded for a precedent,
And many an error by the same example
Will rush into the state: it cannot be.

Shylock
A Daniel come to judgement; yea a Daniel!
O wise young judge, how I do honour thee!

Portia
I pray you let me look upon the bond.

Shylock
Here 'tis, most reverend doctor, here it is.

Portia
Shylock, there's thrice thy money offer'd thee.

Shylock
An oath, an oath. I have an oath in heaven!
Shall I lay perjury upon my soul?
No, not for Venice.

Portia
Why, this bond is forfeit,
And lawfully by this the Jew may claim
A pound of flesh, to be by him cut off
Nearest the merchant's heart. Be merciful:
Take thrice thy money; bid me tear the bond.

233 *tenour*: actual wording.

235 *exposition*: setting-out, explanation.

237 *pillar*: support.

240 *stay*: take my stand.

241 *Most heartily*: with all my heart.

246 *Hath . . . to*: fully authorizes.

249 *elder*: more mature.

253 *balance*: scales.

255 *on your charge*: at your expense.
257 *nominated*: specified.

Shylock
When it is paid, according to the tenour.
It doth appear you are a worthy judge,
You know the law, your exposition
Hath been most sound. I charge you by the law,
Whereof you are a well-deserving pillar,
Proceed to judgement. By my soul I swear
There is no power in the tongue of man
To alter me. I stay here on my bond.

Antonio
Most heartily I do beseech the court
To give the judgement.

Portia
Why then, thus it is:
You must prepare your bosom for his knife.

Shylock
O noble judge, O excellent young man!

Portia
For the intent and purpose of the law
Hath full relation to the penalty
Which here appeareth due upon the bond.

Shylock
'Tis very true. O wise and upright judge,
How much more elder art thou than thy looks!

Portia
Therefore lay bare your bosom

Shylock
Ay, his breast.
So says the bond, doth it not, noble judge?
'Nearest his heart': those are the very words.

Portia
It is so. Are there balance here to weigh
The flesh?

Shylock
I have them ready.

Portia
Have by some surgeon, Shylock, on your charge,
To stop his wounds, lest he do bleed to death.

Shylock
Is it so nominated in the bond?

Portia

It is not so express'd, but what of that?
'Twere good you do so much for charity.

Shylock

I cannot find it; 'tis not in the bond.

Portia

You, merchant: have you anything to say?

Antonio

But little; I am arm'd and well prepar'd.
Give me your hand, Bassanio. Fare you well.
Grieve not that I am fall'n to this for you.
For herein Fortune shows herself more kind
Than is her custom: it is still her use
To let the wretched man outlive his wealth,
To view with hollow eye and wrinkled brow
An age of poverty; from which ling'ring penance
Of such misery doth she cut me off.
Commend me to your honourable wife.
Tell her the process of Antonio's end,
Say how I lov'd you, speak me fair in death,
And when the tale is told, bid her be judge
Whether Bassanio had not once a love.
Repent but you that you shall lose your friend
And he repents not that he pays your debt.
For if the Jew do cut but deep enough
I'll pay it instantly with all my heart.

Bassanio

Antonio, I am married to a wife
Which is as dear to me as life itself;
But life itself, my wife, and all the world,
Are not with me esteem'd above thy life.
I would lose all, ay, sacrifice them all
Here to this devil, to deliver you.

Portia

Your wife would give you little thanks for that
If she were by to hear you make the offer.

Gratiano

I have a wife who I protest I love;
I would she were in heaven, so she could
Entreat some power to change this currish Jew.

262 *arm'd*: i.e. spiritually.

266 *still her use*: usually her custom.

269 *age*: old age.

272 *process*: a) manner; b) legal proceeding.

273 *speak . . . death*: speak kindly of me when I am dead.

276 *Repent but you*: you must only regret.

281 *Which*: who.

285 *deliver*: save.

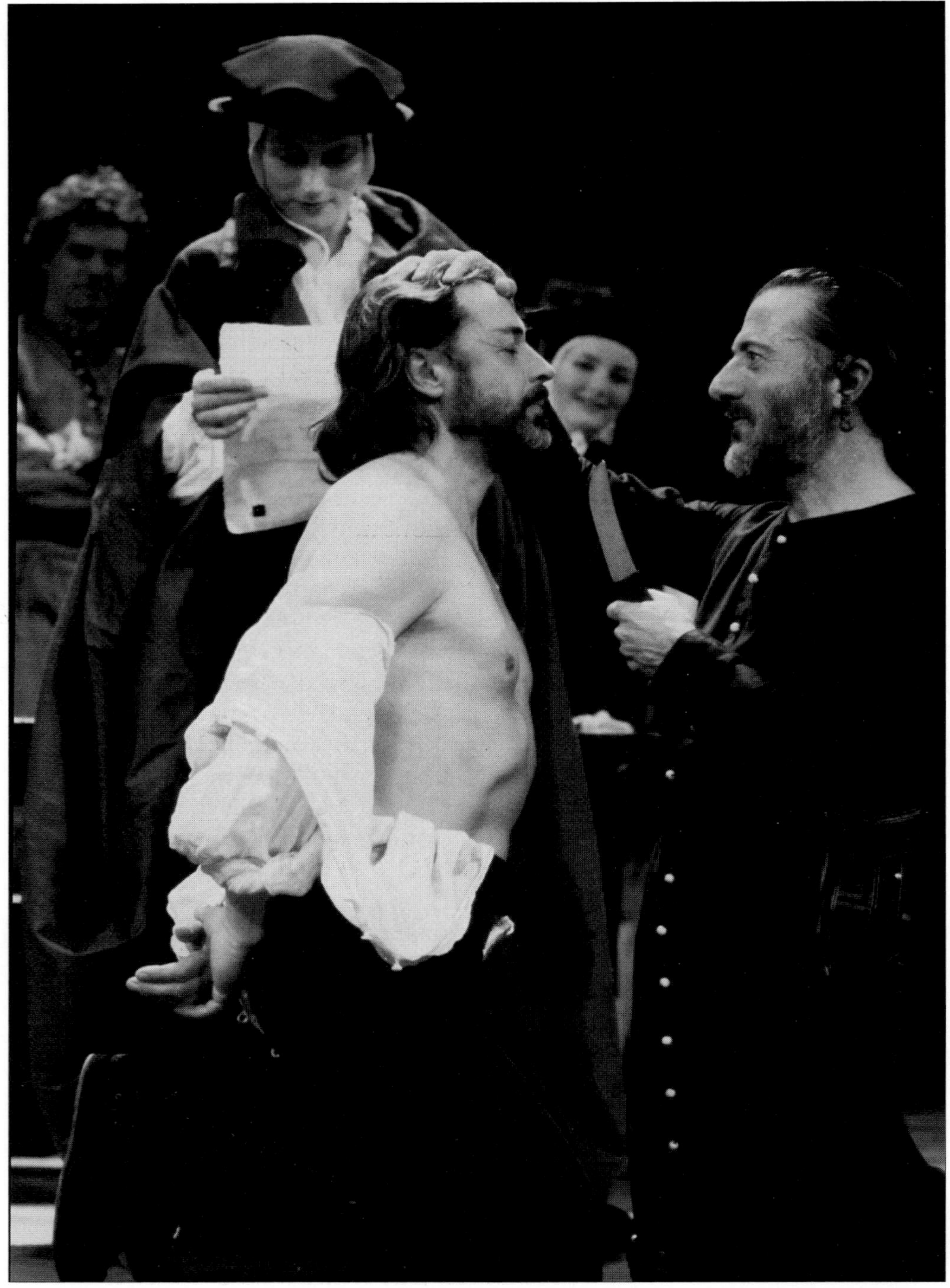

'Most learned judge! A sentence: come, prepare.' (*4*, 1, 302). Geraldine James as Portia, Leigh Lawson as Antonio, and Dustin Hoffman as Shylock, Phoenix Theatre, 1989.

Nerissa
'Tis well you offer it behind her back;
The wish would make else an unquiet house.

Shylock
These be the Christian husbands! I have a daughter:
Would any of the stock of Barabbas
Had been her husband, rather than a Christian!
We trifle time; I pray thee pursue sentence.

Portia
A pound of that same merchant's flesh is thine,
The court awards it, and the law doth give it.

Shylock
Most rightful judge!

Portia
And you must cut this flesh from off his breast;
The law allows it, and the court awards it.

Shylock
Most learned judge! A sentence: come, prepare.

Portia
Tarry a little, there is something else.
This bond doth give thee here no jot of blood.
The words expressly are 'a pound of flesh'.
Take then thy bond, take thou thy pound of flesh,
But in the cutting it, if thou dost shed
One drop of Christian blood, thy lands and goods
Are by the laws of Venice confiscate
Unto the state of Venice.

Gratiano
O upright judge!
Mark, Jew—O learned judge!

Shylock
Is that the law?

Portia
Thyself shall see the Act.
For as thou urgest justice, be assur'd
Thou shalt have justice more than thou desirest.

Gratiano
O learned judge! Mark, Jew: a learned judge.

Shylock
I take this offer then. Pay the bond thrice
And let the Christian go.

294 *stock*: breed.
Barabbas: the thief who was released when Christ was crucified (St John 18:40).
296 *trifle time*: waste time in trivialities.
pursue: go on with.
303 *Tarry*: wait.
304 *jot*: drop.
312 *Act*: the legal act confirming the law.
313 *urgest*: demand.

Bassanio

Here is the money.

Portia

Soft.
The Jew shall have all justice; soft, no haste;
He shall have nothing but the penalty.

Gratiano

O Jew, an upright judge, a learned judge!

Portia

Therefore prepare thee to cut off the flesh.
Shed thou no blood, nor cut thou less nor more
But just a pound of flesh. If thou tak'st more
Or less than a just pound, be it but so much
As makes it light or heavy in the substance
Or the division of the twentieth part
Of one poor scruple—nay, if the scale do turn
But in the estimation of a hair,
Thou diest, and all thy goods are confiscate.

Gratiano

A second Daniel; a Daniel, Jew!
Now, infidel, I have you on the hip.

Portia

Why doth the Jew pause? Take thy forfeiture.

Shylock

Give me my principal, and let me go.

Bassanio

I have it ready for thee; here it is.

Portia

He hath refus'd it in the open court.
He shall have merely justice and his bond.

Gratiano

A Daniel, still say I, a second Daniel!
I thank thee, Jew, for teaching me that word.

Shylock

Shall I not have barely my principal?

Portia

Thou shalt have nothing but the forfeiture,
To be so taken at thy peril, Jew.

Shylock

Why then, the devil give him good of it!
I'll stay no longer question.

321 *upright*: honest.

326 *substance*: weight.

328 *scruple*: a weight unit (used by the old apothecaries) of 20 grains.

329 *estimation*: weight.

332 *on the hip*: at a disadvantage; see *1*, 3, 41.

334 *principal*: the original sum borrowed.

344 *question*: to argue.

Portia

Tarry, Jew:
The law hath yet another hold on you.
It is enacted in the laws of Venice,
If it be prov'd against an alien
That by direct or indirect attempts
He seek the life of any citizen,
The party 'gainst the which he doth contrive
Shall seize one half his goods, the other half
Comes to the privy coffer of the state,
And the offender's life lies in the mercy
Of the duke only, 'gainst all other voice.
In which predicament I say thou stand'st;
For it appears by manifest proceeding
That indirectly, and directly too,
Thou hast contriv'd against the very life
Of the defendant, and thou hast incurr'd
The danger formerly by me rehears'd.
Down, therefore, and beg mercy of the duke.

Gratiano

Beg that thou mayst have leave to hang thyself—
And yet, thy wealth being forfeit to the state,
Thou hast not left the value of a cord;
Therefore thou must be hang'd at the state's charge.

Duke

That thou shalt see the difference of our spirit,
I pardon thee thy life before thou ask it.
For half thy wealth, it is Antonio's;
The other half comes to the general state,
Which humbleness may drive unto a fine.

Portia

Ay, for the state, not for Antonio.

Shylock

Nay, take my life and all, pardon not that:
You take my house when you do take the prop
That doth sustain my house; you take my life
When you do take the means whereby I live.

Portia

What mercy can you render him, Antonio?

Gratiano

A halter gratis—nothing else, for God's sake.

346 *enacted*: decreed.

350 *party*: person (Portia uses the correct legal term, still used today). *contrive*: plot.

351 *seize*: take possession of.

352 *privy coffer*: treasury.

354 *'gainst . . . voice*: without appeal.

356 *manifest proceeding*: quite clearly from what has happened.

360 *rehears'd*: declared.

369 *general state*: general use of the state.

370 *Which . . . fine*: which your good behaviour may reduce to a fine.

371 *not for Antonio*: not Antonio's share of the money.

377 *halter*: rope to hang himself with. *gratis*: free of interest.

Antonio

So please my lord the duke and all the court
To quit the fine for one half of his goods,
I am content, so he will let me have
The other half in use, to render it
Upon his death unto the gentleman
That lately stole his daughter.
Two things provided more: that for this favour
He presently become a Christian;
The other, that he do record a gift,
Here in the court, of all he dies possess'd
Unto his son Lorenzo and his daughter.

Duke

He shall do this, or else I do recant
The pardon that I late pronounced here.

Portia

Art thou contented, Jew? What dost thou say?

Shylock

I am content.

Portia

Clerk, draw a deed of gift.

Shylock

I pray you give me leave to go from hence;
I am not well. Send the deed after me
And I will sign it.

Duke

Get thee gone, but do it.

Gratiano

In christening shalt thou have two godfathers:
Had I been judge, thou shouldst have had ten more
To bring thee to the gallows, not to the font.

[*Exit* Shylock

Duke

Sir, I entreat you home with me to dinner.

Portia

I humbly do desire your grace of pardon.
I must away this night toward Padua,
And it is meet I presently set forth.

---

378 *So please*: if it pleases.

379 *quit*: be satisfied with.
for: instead of.

380 *so*: provided that.

381 *in use*: on trust—to use as Antonio now describes.

385 *presently*: immediately.

386 *record a gift*: sign a legal deed of gift.

387 *all he dies possess'd*: all that he owns when he dies.

389 *recant*: withdraw.

390 *pronounced*: pronouncèd.

396 *godfathers*: sponsors who would guarantee Christian upbringing (for an infant).

397 *ten more*: i.e. enough to constitute a jury.

402 *meet*: necessary.

403 *your leisure serves you not*: you do not have time to spare.
404 *gratify*: show your gratitude to.
405 *bound*: indebted.

407–8 *acquitted Of*: set free from.

408 *in lieu whereof*: in payment for this.

410 *freely*: most willingly.
cope: reward.
pains: trouble.
411 *over and above*: in addition.

416 *mercenary*: interested in money.

417 *know*: recognize.

419 *of force*: it is necessary.
attempt you further: try harder to persuade you.
420 *some remembrance*: something to remind you.
tribute: token of respect.

423 *You press me far*: you are very insistent.
424 *for your sake*: to acknowledge your politeness.
425 *for your love*: to acknowledge your love.

431 *have . . . it*: really want it.

Duke
I am sorry that your leisure serves you not.
Antonio, gratify this gentleman,
For in my mind you are much bound to him.
[*Exit* Duke *and his train*

Bassanio
Most worthy gentleman, I and my friend
Have by your wisdom been this day acquitted
Of grievous penalties, in lieu whereof
Three thousand ducats due unto the Jew
We freely cope your courteous pains withal.

Antonio
And stand indebted over and above
In love and service to you evermore.

Portia
He is well paid that is well satisfied;
And I delivering you am satisfied
And therein do account myself well paid;
My mind was never yet more mercenary.
I pray you know me when we meet again.
I wish you well, and so I take my leave.

Bassanio
Dear sir, of force I must attempt you further.
Take some remembrance of us as a tribute,
Not as a fee. Grant me two things, I pray you:
Not to deny me, and to pardon me.

Portia
You press me far, and therefore I will yield.
Give me your gloves, I'll wear them for your sake;
And for your love I'll take this ring from you.
Do not draw back your hand; I'll take no more,
And you in love shall not deny me this.

Bassanio
This ring, good sir? Alas, it is a trifle;
I will not shame myself to give you this.

Portia
I will have nothing else but only this;
And now methinks I have a mind to it.

Bassanio
There's more depends on this than on the value.

'In christening shalt thou have two godfathers' (*4*, 1, 396). Nicholas Farrell as Bassanio, Antony Sher as Shylock, and Geoffrey Freshwater as Gratiano, Royal Shakespeare Company, 1988.

The dearest ring in Venice will I give you,
And find it out by proclamation.
Only for this I pray you pardon me.

Portia

I see, sir, you are liberal in offers.
You taught me first to beg, and now methinks
You teach me how a beggar should be answer'd.

Bassanio

Good sir, this ring was given me by my wife,
And when she put it on, she made me vow
That I should neither sell, nor give, nor lose it.

Portia

That scuse serves many men to save their gifts;
And if your wife be not a mad woman,
And know how well I have deserv'd this ring,
She would not hold out enemy for ever
For giving it to me. Well, peace be with you.

[*Exeunt* Portia *and* Nerissa

Antonio

My lord Bassanio, let him have the ring.
Let his deservings and my love withal
Be valu'd 'gainst your wife's commandement.

Bassanio

Go, Gratiano, run and overtake him;
Give him the ring, and bring him if thou canst
Unto Antonio's house. Away, make haste.

[*Exit* Gratiano

Come, you and I will thither presently,
And in the morning early will we both
Fly toward Belmont. Come, Antonio. [*Exeunt*

434 *proclamation*: public announcement.

435 *this*: this one.

436 *liberal in offers*: only generous in making offers (without fulfilling them).

442 *scuse*: excuse.

449 *'gainst*: in balance with. *commandement*: commandèment: a four-syllable word is necessary for the rhythm.

Act 4 Scene 2
Portia gets Bassanio's ring—and Nerissa plans to get her own from Gratiano.

1 *Enquire . . . out*: find out where the Jew's house is.
this deed: the document in which he promises to make Lorenzo his heir.

5 *well o'ertane*: I'm glad I've caught up with you.

6 *upon more advice*: having thought more about the matter.

15 *Thou . . . warrant*: I'm sure you'll succeed.
old: extraordinary.

18 *tarry*: wait.

Scene 2

Venice: a street. Enter Portia *and* Nerissa

Portia
Enquire the Jew's house out, give him this deed,
And let him sign it. We'll away tonight
And be a day before our husbands home.
This deed will be well welcome to Lorenzo.

Enter Gratiano

Gratiano
Fair sir, you are well o'ertane.
My lord Bassanio upon more advice
Hath sent you here this ring, and doth entreat
Your company at dinner.

Portia
That cannot be.
His ring I do accept most thankfully,
And so I pray you tell him. Furthermore,
I pray you show my youth old Shylock's house.

Gratiano
That will I do.

Nerissa
[*To* Portia] Sir, I would speak with you.
[*Aside*] I'll see if I can get my husband's ring
Which I did make him swear to keep for ever.

Portia
Thou mayst, I warrant. We shall have old swearing
That they did give the rings away to men;
But we'll outface them, and outswear them too.
—Away, make haste, thou know'st where I will tarry.

Nerissa
Come, good sir, will you show me to this house?

[*Exeunt*

ACT 5

Act 5 Scene 1
Lorenzo teases Jessica as they wait in the moonlight. Portia and Nerissa return from Venice, followed by Bassanio and Gratiano—who are embarrassed when their wives demand to see the rings. All is explained, and Portia has good news for Antonio.

SCENE 1

Belmont: the garden. Enter Lorenzo *and* Jessica

Lorenzo
The moon shines bright. In such a night as this,
When the sweet wind did gently kiss the trees,
And they did make no noise, in such a night
Troilus methinks mounted the Troyan walls
And sigh'd his soul toward the Grecian tents,
Where Cressid lay that night.

Jessica
In such a night
Did Thisbe fearfully o'ertrip the dew,
And saw the lion's shadow ere himself,
And ran dismay'd away.

Lorenzo
In such a night
Stood Dido with a willow in her hand
Upon the wild sea banks, and waft her love
To come again to Carthage.

Jessica
In such a night
Medea gather'd the enchanted herbs
That did renew old Aeson.

Lorenzo
In such a night
Did Jessica steal from the wealthy Jew
And with an unthrift love did run from Venice
As far as Belmont.

Jessica
In such a night
Did young Lorenzo swear he lov'd her well,
Stealing her soul with many vows of faith,
And ne'er a true one.

4–6 *Troilus . . . night*: In the Trojan War Troilus was separated from Cressida when she was taken to the Greek camp; their love is the subject of Chaucer's *Troylus and Criseyde* and Shakespeare's *Troilus and Cressida*.
7, 10, 13 *Thisbe . . . Dido . . . Medea*: Their stories are told in Chaucer's *Legend of Good Women*.
7 *Thisbe*: When Thisbe, frightened by a lion, failed to keep her assignation, her grieving lover Pyramus killed himself; a (comic) version of the episode is presented in *A Midsummer's Night's Dream*.
o'ertrip: trip across.
8 *ere himself*: before she saw him.
10 *Dido*: The Queen of Carthage, deserted by her lover Aeneas, was the protagonist of a tragedy by Shakespeare's contemporary, Christopher Marlowe.
willow: The traditional emblem of forsaken love.
11 *waft*: beckoned.
13–14 *Medea . . . Aeson*: When she had helped Jason on his voyage to win the Golden Fleece (see *1*, 1, 170 note), the enchantress Medea gave Aeson, his father, a rejuvenating herbal potion.
15 *steal*: a) creep away; b) rob.
16 *unthrift*: a) careless, prodigal; b) penniless.
19 *Stealing her soul*: a) gaining possession of her love; b) converting her away from her Jewish faith.

'In such a night Did Jessica steal from the wealthy Jew' (*5*, 1, 14–15). Paul Spence as Lorenzo and Deborah Goodman as Jessica, Royal Shakespeare Company, 1987.

Lorenzo

In such a night
Did pretty Jessica (like a little shrew)
Slander her love, and he forgave it her.

Jessica

I would outnight you, did nobody come:
But hark, I hear the footing of a man.

21 *shrew*: scolding woman.

23 *outnight you*: i.e. beat you at this game.
did nobody come: if there were not somebody coming.

Enter Stephano, *a messenger*

Lorenzo

Who comes so fast in silence of the night?

Stephano

A friend.

Lorenzo

A friend? What friend? Your name, I pray you, friend?

Stephano

Stephano is my name, and I bring word
My mistress will before the break of day
Be here at Belmont. She doth stray about
By holy crosses where she kneels and prays
For happy wedlock hours.

Lorenzo

Who comes with her?

Stephano

None but a holy hermit and her maid.
I pray you, is my master yet return'd?

Lorenzo

He is not, nor we have not heard from him.
But go we in, I pray thee, Jessica,
And ceremoniously let us prepare
Some welcome for the mistress of the house.

30–2 *She . . . hours*: This apparent change of plan (*3*, 4, 26–32) passes unnoticed in the theatre.
31 *holy crosses*: wayside shrines.

37–8 *ceremoniously . . . welcome*: let us prepare some ceremony of welcome.

Enter Lancelot, *the Clown*

Lancelot

Sola, sola! Wo ha, ho! Sola, sola!

Lorenzo

Who calls?

39 *Sola . . . sola*: Lancelot pretends that he cannot find Lorenzo.

Lancelot
Sola! Did you see Master Lorenzo? Master Lorenzo, sola, sola!

Lorenzo
Leave holloaing, man! Here!

Lancelot
Sola! Where, where?

Lorenzo
Here!

Lancelot
Tell him there's a post come from my master, with his horn full of good news: my master will be here ere morning, sweet soul.

Lorenzo
Let's in and there expect their coming.
And yet no matter: why should we go in?
My friend Stephano, signify I pray you,
Within the house, your mistress is at hand,
And bring your music forth into the air.
[*Exit* Stephano

How sweet the moonlight sleeps upon this bank!
Here will we sit, and let the sounds of music
Creep in our ears; soft stillness and the night
Become the touches of sweet harmony.
Sit, Jessica. Look how the floor of heaven
Is thick inlaid with patens of bright gold.
There's not the smallest orb which thou behold'st
But in his motion like an angel sings,
Still choiring to the young-eyed cherubins.
Such harmony is in immortal souls,
But whilst this muddy vesture of decay
Doth grossly close it in, we cannot hear it.

Enter Stephano *with musicians*

Come, ho! and wake Diana with a hymn.
With sweetest touches pierce your mistress' ear,
And draw her home with music.

Music plays

43 *Leave holloaing*: stop shouting.

46 *post*: courier.

47 *horn . . . news*: i.e. like a cornucopia (= horn of plenty).

48 *sweet soul*: Many editors place these words at the beginning of line 49 (which is two syllables short of a regular pentameter).

51 *signify*: announce.

53 *your music*: the resident musicians.

57 *Become*: suit, befit.

59 *patens*: little metal plates (used in Holy Communion).

60–1 *There's . . . sings*: The Elizabethans believed that heavenly harmony was created by the movement of the planets ('orbs').

62 *Still choiring*: always singing together. *young-eyed cherubins*: Elizabethans imagined these angelic creatures (see Ezekiel 10:12) as beautiful winged children.

63 *Such*: the same.

64 *muddy . . . decay*: clothing of mortality made from the dust of the earth (Genesis 2:7).

65 *grossly*: roughly, crudely.

66 *wake Diana*: call out the moon (which seems in line 109 to have gone behind a cloud).

Jessica

I am never merry when I hear sweet music.

Lorenzo

The reason is your spirits are attentive.
For do but note a wild and wanton herd
Or race of youthful and unhandled colts
Fetching mad bounds, bellowing and neighing loud—
Which is the hot condition of their blood—
If they but hear perchance a trumpet sound,
Or any air of music touch their ears,
You shall perceive them make a mutual stand,
Their savage eyes turn'd to a modest gaze
By the sweet power of music. Therefore the poet
Did feign that Orpheus drew trees, stones, and floods;
Since naught so stockish, hard, and full of rage,
But music for the time doth change his nature.
The man that hath no music in himself,
Nor is not mov'd with concord of sweet sounds,
Is fit for treasons, stratagems, and spoils;
The motions of his spirit are dull as night
And his affections dark as Erebus.
Let no such man be trusted. Mark the music.

Enter Portia *and* Nerissa

Portia

That light we see is burning in my hall.
How far that little candle throws his beams!
So shines a good deed in a naughty world.

Nerissa

When the moon shone we did not see the candle.

Portia

So doth the greater glory dim the less:
A substitute shines brightly as a king
Until a king be by, and then his state
Empties itself, as doth an inland brook
Into the main of waters. Music, hark!

Nerissa

It is your music, madam, of the house.

72 *race*: herd, stud.
unhandled: unbroken, untrained.
74 *hot . . . blood*: nature of their excited spirit.
75 *perchance*: perhaps.
77 *make . . . stand*: all stand still at once.
78 *modest*: gentle.
79–80 *the poet . . . floods*: the Roman poet Ovid told how Orpheus, a Greek musician, charmed even lifeless objects with his music.
81 *naught*: nothing.
stockish: stubborn.
84 *concord*: harmony.
85 *stratagems*: plots.
spoils: destruction.
86 *motions*: movements.
87 *Erebus*: the place of darkness in the classical underworld.
88 *Mark*: pay attention to.
91 *naughty*: wicked.
94 *substitute*: deputy.
95 *by*: present.
95–6 *his . . . itself*: his glory vanishes.
97 *main of waters*: sea.
98 *your . . . house*: the resident musicians.

Portia

99 *Nothing . . . respect*: i.e. everything is relative to something else.

Nothing is good, I see, without respect;
Methinks it sounds much sweeter than by day.

Nerissa

101 *virtue*: special quality.

Silence bestows that virtue on it, madam.

Portia

103 *attended*: listened to.

104 *nightingale*: A bird that sings only at night, when all other birds are silent.

107 *by . . . are*: are given a better flavour by coming at the proper time.

109 *the moon . . . Endymion*: Diana, goddess of the moon, slept on Mount Latmos with her love, the shepherd-boy Endymion.

The crow doth sing as sweetly as the lark
When neither is attended; and I think
The nightingale, if she should sing by day
When every goose is cackling, would be thought
No better a musician than the wren.
How many things by season season'd are
To their right praise and true perfection.
Peace, ho! The moon sleeps with Endymion
And would not be awak'd!

Music ceases

Lorenzo

That is the voice
Or I am much deceiv'd, of Portia!

Portia

He knows me as the blind man knows the cuckoo
By the bad voice.

Lorenzo

Dear lady, welcome home!

Portia

115 *speed*: prosper.

We have been praying for our husbands' welfare,
Which speed we hope the better for our words.
Are they return'd?

Lorenzo

Madam, they are not yet.
But there is come a messenger before
To signify their coming.

Portia

119–20 *take . . . note*: make no mention.

Go in, Nerissa:
Give order to my servants that they take
No note at all of our being absent hence—
Nor you, Lorenzo, Jessica nor you.

121s.d. *tucket*: personal trumpet call.

A tucket sounds

Lorenzo
Your husband is at hand, I hear his trumpet.
We are no telltales, madam; fear you not.

Portia
This night methinks is but the daylight sick,
It looks a little paler; 'tis a day
Such as the day is when the sun is hid.

Enter Bassanio, Antonio, Gratiano, *and their followers*

Bassanio
We should hold day with the Antipodes,
If you would walk in absence of the sun.

Portia
Let me give light, but let me not be light,
For a light wife doth make a heavy husband,
And never be Bassanio so for me—
But God sort all! You are welcome home, my lord.

Bassanio
I thank you, madam. Give welcome to my friend.
This is the man, this is Antonio,
To whom I am so infinitely bound.

Portia
You should in all sense be much bound to him,
For as I hear he was much bound for you.

Antonio
No more than I am well acquitted of.

Portia
Sir, you are very welcome to our house.
It must appear in other ways than words:
Therefore I scant this breathing courtesy.

Gratiano
[*To* Nerissa] By yonder moon I swear you do me wrong!
In faith, I gave it to the judge's clerk,
Would he were gelt that had it, for my part,
Since you do take it, love, so much at heart.

Portia
A quarrel ho, already! What's the matter?

127–8 *We . . . sun*: if you were to walk at night, it would be daylight here as well as on the other side of the globe ('the Antipodes').

129 *be light*: be faithless.

130 *heavy*: sorrowful.

131 *for me*: because of what I have done.

132 *sort all*: decide everything.

135 *bound*: indebted.

137 *bound*: in chains as a prisoner.

138 *acquitted of*: repaid for (with the love of Bassanio).

141 *scant*: cut short.
breathing courtesy: verbal politeness.

144 *Would . . . gelt*: I wish he had been castrated.

145 *take . . . heart*: care so much about it.

Gratiano
About a hoop of gold, a paltry ring
That she did give me, whose poesy was
For all the world like cutler's poetry
Upon a knife: 'Love me, and leave me not.'

Nerissa
What talk you of the poesy or the value?
You swore to me when I did give it you,
That you would wear it till your hour of death,
And that it should lie with you in your grave.
Though not for me, yet for your vehement oaths
You should have been respective and have kept it.
Gave it a judge's clerk! No, God's my judge
The clerk will ne'er wear hair on's face that had it.

Gratiano
He will, and if he live to be a man.

Nerissa
Ay, if a woman live to be a man.

Gratiano
Now by this hand, I gave it to a youth,
A kind of boy, a little scrubbed boy
No higher than thyself, the judge's clerk,
A prating boy that begg'd it as a fee;
I could not for my heart deny it him.

Portia
You were to blame, I must be plain with you,
To part so slightly with your wife's first gift,
A thing stuck on with oaths upon your finger
And so riveted with faith unto your flesh.
I gave my love a ring, and made him swear
Never to part with it, and here he stands.
I dare be sworn for him he would not leave it
Nor pluck it from his finger for the wealth
That the world masters. Now in faith, Gratiano,
You give your wife too unkind a cause of grief;
And 'twere to me, I should be mad at it.

Bassanio
[*Aside*] Why, I were best to cut my left hand off
And swear I lost the ring defending it.

Gratiano
My lord Bassanio gave his ring away

148 *poesy*: motto engraved inside a ring.

149 *cutler's poetry*: doggerel verse inscribed on a knife-handle.

151 *What*: why.

155 *for me*: for my sake.

158 *wear hair on's face*: grow a beard.

159 *and if*: if ever.

162 *scrubbed*: scrubbèd; stunted.

164 *prating*: chattering.

172 *leave*: part with.

174 *masters*: is master of.

176 *And 'twere to me*: if it had been done to me.

Unto the judge that begg'd it, and indeed
Deserv'd it too; and then the boy his clerk
That took some pains in writing, he begg'd mine,
And neither man nor master would take aught
But the two rings.

Portia

What ring gave you, my lord?
Not that, I hope, which you receiv'd of me?

Bassanio

If I could add a lie unto a fault,
I would deny it; but you see my finger
Hath not the ring upon it, it is gone.

Portia

Even so void is your false heart of truth.
By heaven, I will ne'er come in your bed
Until I see the ring.

Nerissa

Nor I in yours
Till I again see mine.

Bassanio

Sweet Portia,
If you did know to whom I gave the ring,
If you did know for whom I gave the ring,
And would conceive for what I gave the ring,
And how unwillingly I left the ring,
When naught would be accepted but the ring,
You would abate the strength of your displeasure.

Portia

If you had known the virtue of the ring,
Or half her worthiness that gave the ring,
Or your own honour to contain the ring,
You would not then have parted with the ring.
What man is there so much unreasonable,
If you had pleas'd to have defended it
With any terms of zeal, wanted the modesty
To urge the thing held as a ceremony?
Nerissa teaches me what to believe:
I'll die for't, but some woman had the ring!

Bassanio

No by my honour, madam, by my soul
No woman had it, but a civil doctor,

182 *pains*: care.

189 *void*: empty.

199–202 *If . . . ring*: Portia parodies Bassanio's figure of speech (epistrophe).
199 *virtue*: special quality.
201 *contain*: keep.

205 *terms of zeal*: determination.
205–6 *wanted . . . ceremony*: would have been so indelicate to press for something held sacred.
208 *I'll die for't*: I am ready to die for my belief.

210 *civil doctor*: doctor of civil law.

213 *suffer'd*: allowed.
214 *held up*: saved.
217 *beset*: overcome.
219 *besmear*: stain.
220 *blessed*: blessèd.
candles of the night: the stars.
222 *of*: from.
230 *Lie . . . home*: don't spend a single night away from home.
Argus: A monster of classical mythology who closed only two of his hundred eyes at any one time.
232 *yet mine own*: still intact.
234 *be well advis'd*: take good care.
235 *to mine own protection*: to look after my own honour.
236 *take*: catch.
237 *I'll mar . . . pen*: I'll ruin his equipment.
240 *enforced*: enforcèd.

Which did refuse three thousand ducats of me,
And begg'd the ring, the which I did deny him,
And suffer'd him to go displeas'd away,
Even he that had held up the very life
Of my dear friend. What should I say, sweet lady?
I was enforc'd to send it after him;
I was beset with shame and courtesy;
My honour would not let ingratitude
So much besmear it. Pardon me, good lady,
For by these blessed candles of the night,
Had you been there I think you would have begg'd
The ring of me to give the worthy doctor.

Portia

Let not that doctor e'er come near my house.
Since he hath got the jewel that I lov'd
And that which you did swear to keep for me,
I will become as liberal as you;
I'll not deny him anything I have,
No, not my body, nor my husband's bed:
Know him I shall, I am well sure of it.
Lie not a night from home. Watch me like Argus.
If you do not, if I be left alone,
Now by mine honour which is yet mine own,
I'll have that doctor for my bedfellow.

Nerissa

And I his clerk; therefore be well advis'd
How you do leave me to mine own protection.

Gratiano

Well, do you so. Let not me take him then,
For if I do, I'll mar the young clerk's pen.

Antonio

I am th'unhappy subject of these quarrels.

Portia

Sir, grieve not you; you are welcome notwithstanding.

Bassanio

Portia, forgive me this enforced wrong;
And in the hearing of these many friends
I swear to thee, even by thine own fair eyes
Wherein I see myself—

Portia

Mark you but that?

In both my eyes he doubly sees himself:
In each eye one. Swear by your double self,
And there's an oath of credit!

Bassanio

Nay, but hear me.
Pardon this fault, and by my soul I swear
I nevermore will break an oath with thee.

Antonio

I once did lend my body for his wealth,
Which but for him that had your husband's ring
Had quite miscarried. I dare be bound again,
My soul upon the forfeit, that your lord
Will nevermore break faith advisedly.

Portia

Then you shall be his surety. Give him this,
And bid him keep it better than the other.

Antonio

Here, Lord Bassanio, swear to keep this ring.

Bassanio

By heaven, it is the same I gave the doctor!

Portia

I had it of him; pardon me, Bassanio,
For by this ring the doctor lay with me.

Nerissa

And pardon me, my gentle Gratiano,
For that same scrubbed boy the doctor's clerk,
In lieu of this, last night did lie with me.

Gratiano

Why, this is like the mending of highways
In summer where the ways are fair enough!
What, are we cuckolds ere we have deserv'd it?

Portia

Speak not so grossly; you are all amaz'd.
Here is a letter, read it at your leisure;
It comes from Padua, from Bellario.
There you shall find that Portia was the doctor,
Nerissa there her clerk. Lorenzo here
Shall witness I set forth as soon as you,
And even but now return'd; I have not yet
Enter'd my house. Antonio, you are welcome;
And I have better news in store for you

245 *double*: a) two-fold; b) two-faced.
246 *of credit*: that can be believed.
249 *wealth*: well-being, happiness.
251 *miscarried*: been lost.
252 *My . . . forfeit*: at the risk of forfeiting my soul.
253 *advisedly*: knowingly.
254 *surety*: security.
261 *scrubbed*: scrubbèd.
262 *In lieu of*: in return for.
263–4 *mending . . . enough*: repairing good roads unnecessarily in summertime; Gratiano is saying that this situation is ridiculous.
265 *cuckolds*: men whose wives are unfaithful to them.
deserv'd it: i.e. by showing themselves to be unsatisfactory lovers.
266 *grossly*: crudely.
amaz'd: bewildered.

Than you expect. Unseal this letter soon;
There you shall find three of your argosies
Are richly come to harbour suddenly.
You shall not know by what strange accident
I chanced on this letter.

Antonio

I am dumb.

Bassanio

Were you the doctor and I knew you not?

Gratiano

Were you the clerk that is to make me cuckold?

Nerissa

Ay, but the clerk that never means to do it,
Unless he live until he be a man.

Bassanio

Sweet doctor, you shall be my bedfellow;
When I am absent, then lie with my wife.

Antonio

Sweet lady, you have given me life and living;
For here I read for certain that my ships
Are safely come to road.

Portia

How now, Lorenzo?
My clerk hath some good comforts too for you.

Nerissa

Ay, and I'll give them him without a fee.
There do I give to you and Jessica
From the rich Jew, a special deed of gift
After his death of all he dies possess'd of.

Lorenzo

Fair ladies, you drop manna in the way
Of starved people.

Portia

It is almost morning;
And yet I am sure you are not satisfied
Of these events at full. Let us go in,
And charge us there upon inter'gatories,
And we will answer all things faithfully.

Gratiano

Let it be so. The first inter'gatory
That my Nerissa shall be sworn on is:

275 *soon*: quickly.

279 *chanced*: chancèd.

288 *road*: anchorage.

294 *manna*: the food from heaven that sustained the Israelites starving in the desert (Exodus 16:14–15).

295 *starved*: starvèd.

297 *at full*: in detail.

298 *charge . . . inter'gatories*: interrogate us on oath.

305 *couching*: going to bed.
306 *while I live*: as long as I live.
306–7 *I'll . . . ring*: I'll take care of nothing so much as guarding Nerissa's ring (and also her honour).

Whether till the next night she had rather stay,
Or go to bed now, being two hours to day.
But were the day come, I should wish it dark,
Till I were couching with the doctor's clerk.
Well, while I live I'll fear no other thing
So sore as keeping safe Nerissa's ring. [*Exeunt*

male | female
Venice | Belmont
business | romance
violence | serenity/music
day | night/moonlit
reason | emotion
clarity | mystery
menstruation
disguise

moon-white, purity

Sources

The lady, the pound of flesh, and the ring

The most likely source for the main plot in *The Merchant of Venice* seems to have been one of the stories in *Il Pecorone* (= 'the big sheep', or dunce), a collection of tales by Ser Giovanni of Florence, which was published at Milan in 1558. No English version has ever been found—so we must assume that Shakespeare read the original in Italian.

Ansaldo, a wealthy merchant of Venice, financed his godson Giannetto in his attempts to win the Lady of Belmont. This Lady was a rich widow who had agreed to marry the first man who succeeded in making love to her—but she had imposed the condition that all unsuccessful lovers must forfeit everything they possessed. Giannetto twice attempted this task; and both times he failed—because he was given drugged wine to make him fall asleep before the lady came to bed. Because he was ashamed of his failures, he told Ansaldo that he had twice been shipwrecked. Determined to make a third attempt, he begged Ansaldo for more money. This time Ansaldo was forced to borrow ten thousand ducats from a Jew to enable him to equip yet another ship for Giannetto. The Jew made the condition that if the loan were not repaid upon St John's Day, the merchant would forfeit a pound of his own flesh.

Giannetto (warned by a maid not to drink the drugged wine) succeeded in making love to the lady; he married her, and was proclaimed sovereign of all that she possessed. He forgot about Ansaldo's bargain with the Jew until St John's Day arrived, and then he told his wife the whole story. The Lady sent Giannetto to Venice with enough money to repay the Jew; and she herself followed him, disguised as a lawyer.

The Jew refused to accept Giannetto's money, because he wanted to say that he had killed the greatest of all the Christian merchants. The 'lawyer' claimed that she could settle all disputes, and she heard the Jew's case against Ansaldo, with Giannetto's offer to repay the debt. She advised the Jew to take the ten thousand ducats, but he persisted in refusing. She then told him to take the pound of flesh—but, at the last moment, she warned him that if he took more than an exact pound, or shed one drop of blood, he would be executed. The Jew then asked for the money instead of the flesh. When this was refused, he tore up the bond.

Gianetto offered the ducats as a fee to the 'lawyer', but she demanded to be given his ring. He then returned to Belmont, taking Ansaldo with him. The Lady accused Giannetto of giving the ring to one of his former mistresses. He wept, but finally the Lady explained everything—and Ansaldo married the maid who had warned Giannetto about the drugged wine.

The caskets

The casket story may have been suggested by the account in History 32 of *Gesta Romanorum*, translated by R. Robinson in 1595, where the heroine was told to make a choice between three 'vessels' in order to win a husband.

'The first [vessel] was made of pure gold, well-beset with precious stones without, and within full of dead mens' bones; and thereupon was engraved this poesy: *Whoso chooseth me shall find that he deserveth.* The second vessel was made of fine silver, filled with earth and worms; and the superscription was thus: *Whoso chooseth me shall find that his nature desireth.* The third vessel was made of lead, full within of precious stones; and thereupon was ensculped this poesy: *Whoso chooseth me, shall find that God hath disposed for him.*'

The Jew and his daughter

A contemporary play, *The Jew of Malta* (*c.* 1589) by Christopher Marlowe, gave Shakespeare some inspiration for the character of Shylock. Marlowe's Jew, Barabas, is determined to be revenged on the Christians who persecute him; and he too has a daughter who loves a Christian. Shylock's lament—'My daughter! O my ducats! O my daughter!' (2, 8, 15)—seems to be modelled on Barabas's cry: 'Oh my girl! My gold, my fortune . . . Oh girl! Oh gold! Oh beauty! Oh my bliss!' (2, 2, 47–54).

Classwork and Examinations

The works of Shakespeare are studied all over the world, and this classroom edition is being used in many different countries. Teaching methods vary from school to school—even *within* the United Kingdom—and there are many different ways of examining a student's work. Some teachers and examiners expect detailed knowledge of Shakespeare's text; others ask for imaginative involvement with his characters and their situations; and there are some teachers who want their students, by means of 'workshop' activities, to share in the theatrical experience of directing and performing a play. Most people use a variety of methods. This section of the book offers a few suggestions for approaches to *The Merchant of Venice* which could be used in schools and colleges to help with students' understanding and *enjoyment* of the play.

A Discussion of Themes and Topics
B Character Study
C Activities
D Context Questions
E Critical Appreciation
F Essays
G Projects

A Discussion of Themes and Topics

Talking about the play—about the issues it raises and the characters who are involved—is one of the most rewarding and pleasurable aspects of the study of Shakespeare. It makes sense to discuss each scene as it is read, sharing impressions—and perhaps correcting misapprehensions. It can be useful to compare aspects of this play with other fictions—plays, novels, films—or with modern life. A large class can divide into small groups, each with a leader, who can discuss different aspects of a single topic and then report back to the main assembly.

Suggestions

A1 Bassanio borrows money from Antonio, and Antonio borrows from Shylock. Antonio disapproves of Shylock because he charges interest on his loans; and Shylock grumbles because Antonio 'lends out money gratis' (1, 3, 39). What is *your* attitude to borrowing and lending?

A2 Portia's father, even though he is dead, has power over his daughter's choice of husband—'the will of a living daughter is curbed by the will of a dead father' (*1*, 2, 23–4). Do you think that parents—alive or dead—should have any influence over their children's marriages?

A3 Jessica, a Jew, marries Lorenzo, a Christian; do you approve of such 'mixed' marriages?

A4 'All things that are, Are with more spirit chased than enjoy'd' (*2*, 6, 13–14). How true is this?

A5 Shylock demands justice, but Portia advocates mercy (*Act 4*, Scene 1). Discuss justice and mercy in the world at the beginning of the twenty-first century.

A6 Consider the possibilities of staging this play in settings other than seventeenth century England.

B Character Study

Shakespeare's characters can be studied in many different ways, either from the *outside*, where the detached, critical student (or group of students) can see the function of every character within the whole scheme and pattern of the play; or from the *inside*, where the sympathetic student (like an actor) can identify with a single character and can look at the action and the other characters from his/her point of view. The two methods—both useful in different ways—are really complementary to each other.

Suggestions

a) from 'outside' the character

B1 Is it possible to characterize Salarino and Solanio? What is their function in the play?

B2 'I have much ado to know myself' (Antonio, *1*, 1, 7). How well do we get to *know* Antonio?

B3 Do you find Bassanio an attractive—and *coherent*—character?

B4 Describe the character of Gratiano, and say what you think he contributes to the play.

B5 Does the play need Lancelot Gobbo and his father?

B6 How sympathetic are you to Shylock?

b) from 'inside' the character

B7 In the character of Antonio, speak your thoughts in soliloquy at the end of *Act 1*, Scene 1, or confide them to your diary.

B8 As Bassanio, give your reasons—in a modern idiom—for your choice of caskets.

B9 Imagine that you are a servant who is present when one of the caskets is opened. Describe the scene, and the characters involved, in a letter to your friend.

B10 Write a letter from Jessica to her girl-friend, recounting her adventures with Lorenzo.

B11 In the character of Nerissa, describe how you went to the court in Venice and what it was that you saw and heard there.

C Activities

These can involve two or more students, preferably working *away from* the desk or study-table and using gesture and position ('body-language') as well as speech. They can help students to develop a sense of drama and the dramatic aspects of Shakespeare's play—which was written to be *performed*, not studied in a classroom.

Suggestions

C1 Speak the lines—act the scenes! To familiarize yourselves with Shakespeare's verse, try different reading techniques—reading by punctuation marks (where each person hands over to the next at every punctuation mark); reading by sentences; and reading by speeches. Begin acting with small units—about ten lines—where two or three characters are speaking to each other; rehearse these in groups of students, and perform them before the whole class. Read the lines from a script—then act them out in your own words.

C2 Devise a scene for Salarino and Solanio in which they can discuss Antonio's strange moods.

C3 The engagement of Gratiano and Nerissa seems to take everyone by surprise at the end of *Act 3*, Scene 2. Plan a scene (or scenes) to show how their love develops.

C4 Arraign Antonio before the Race Relations Board.

C5 The trial of Antonio is a very important event in Venice. Give it full 'media coverage'—newspaper, radio, and television (with signing for the deaf, if possible).

D Context Questions

Questions like these, which are sometimes used in written examinations, can also be helpful as a class revision quiz, testing knowledge of the play and some understanding of its words.

D1 The patch is kind enough, but a huge feeder,
Snail-slow in profit, and he sleeps by day
More than the wildcat. Drones hive not with me,
Therefore I part with him, and part with him
To one that I would have him help to waste
His borrow'd purse.

(i) Who is speaking, and to whom does he speak?
(ii) Who is being discussed, and what has this person decided to do?
(iii) How does the person addressed feel towards the speaker?

D2 You know me well, and herein spend but time
To wind about my love with circumstance;
And out of doubt you do me now more wrong
In making question of my uttermost
Than if you had made waste of all I have.
Then do but say to me what I should do

(i) Who is speaking, and to whom does he speak?
(ii) What is the speaker accusing the other person of?
(iii) What does the person addressed want the speaker to do, and why?

D3 O, be thou damn'd, inexecrable dog,
And for thy life let justice be accus'd!
Thou almost mak'st me waver in my faith,
To hold opinion with Pythagoras
That souls of animals infuse themselves
Into the trunks of men. Thy currish spirit
Govern'd a wolf

(i) Who is speaking, and on what occasion?
(ii) What has the person addressed been doing to cause this outburst?
(iii) What effect does this speech have on the person addressed?

D4 Lock up my doors, and when you hear the drum
And the vile squealing of the wry-neck'd fife,
Clamber not you up to the casements then
Nor thrust your head into the public street

To gaze on Christian fools with varnish'd faces;
But stop my house's ears—I mean my casements—
Let not the sound of shallow foppery enter
My sober house.

(i) Who is speaking, and to whom does he speak?
(ii) Where is the speaker going?
(iii) How will the 'Christian fools with varnish'd faces' help the person addressed?

D5 You swore to me when I did give it you,
That you would wear it till your hour of death,
And that it should lie with you in your grave.
Though not for me, yet for your vehement oaths
You should have been respective and have kept it.
Gave it a judge's clerk! No, God's my judge
The clerk will ne'er wear hair on's face that had it.

(i) Two people are quarrelling: who are they?
(ii) What does 'it' refer to?
(iii) Will the 'clerk' ever 'wear hair' on his face? Why?

D6 I am as like to call thee so again,
To spit on thee again, to spurn thee too.
If thou wilt lend this money, lend it not
As to thy friends, for when did friendship take
A breed for barren metal of his friend?
But lend it rather to thine enemy,
Who if he break, thou may'st with better face
Exact the penalty.

(i) Who is speaking, and to whom does he speak?
(ii) Why will the speaker spit on the man he addresses?
(iii) What is meant by 'if he break'? Will the speaker ever 'break'?

E Critical Appreciation These present passages from the play and ask questions about them. Some examination boards allow candidates to take their copies of the play into the examination room, asking them to re-read specified sections of the play (such as the ones printed here) and answer questions on them.

E1 **Portia** (*Act 3*, Scene 2, lines 149–74)
You see me, Lord Bassanio, where I stand,
Such as I am. Though for myself alone

I would not be ambitious in my wish
To wish myself much better, yet for you
I would be trebled twenty times myself,
A thousand times more fair, ten thousand times
More rich, that only to stand high in your account
I might in virtues, beauties, livings, friends,
Exceed account. But the full sum of me
Is sum of something: which to term in gross
Is an unlesson'd girl, unschool'd, unpractis'd;
Happy in this, she is not yet so old
But she may learn; happier than this,
She is not bred so dull but she can learn;
Happiest of all, is that her gentle spirit
Commits itself to yours to be directed
As from her lord, her governor, her king.
Myself, and what is mine, to you and yours
Is now converted. But now I was the lord
Of this fair mansion, master of my servants,
Queen o'er myself; and even now, but now,
This house, these servants, and this same myself
Are yours, my lord's. I give them with this ring,
Which when you part from, lose, or give away,
Let it presage the ruin of your love,
And be my vantage to exclaim on you.

What impression of the relationship between Portia and Bassanio do you get from this passage? How has the play prepared you for this moment?

E2 **The Prince of Arragon** (*Act 2*, Scene 9, lines 30–51)

I will not choose what many men desire,
Because I will not jump with common spirits,
And rank me with the barbarous multitudes.
Why then, to thee, thou silver treasure house:
Tell me once more what title thou dost bear.
'Who chooseth me, shall get as much as he deserves.'
And well said too, for who shall go about
To cozen Fortune and be honourable
Without the stamp of merit? Let none presume
To wear an undeserved dignity.
O, that estates, degrees, and offices
Were not deriv'd corruptly, and that clear honour

Were purchas'd by the merit of the wearer!
How many then should cover that stand bare!
How many be commanded that command!
How much low peasantry would then be glean'd
From the true seed of honour, and how much honour
Pick'd from the chaff and ruin of the times
To be new varnish'd! Well, but to my choice.
'Who chooseth me, shall get as much as he deserves.'
I will assume desert. Give me a key for this,
And instantly unlock my fortunes here.

Describe the character of the Prince of Arragon as it is revealed in this speech and elsewhere in his scene with Portia. What is the dramatic importance of this second opening of the caskets?

E3 **Lorenzo** (*Act* 5, Scene 1, lines 54–68)

How sweet the moonlight sleeps upon this bank!
Here will we sit, and let the sounds of music
Creep in our ears; soft stillness and the night
Become the touches of sweet harmony.
Sit, Jessica. Look how the floor of heaven
Is thick inlaid with patens of bright gold.
There's not the smallest orb which thou behold'st
But in his motion like an angel sings,
Still choiring to the young-eyed cherubins.
Such harmony is in immortal souls,
But whilst this muddy vesture of decay
Doth grossly close it in, we cannot hear it.
Enter Stephano *with musicians*
Come, ho! and wake Diana with a hymn.
With sweetest touches pierce your mistress' ear,
And draw her home with music.

What is the dramatic function of these lines? How does Shakespeare help the audience to recover from the emotions of the trial scene?

F Essays

These will usually give you a specific topic to discuss, or perhaps a question that must be answered, in writing, *with a reasoned argument.* They *never* want you to tell the story of the play—so don't! Your examiner—or teacher—has read the play, and does not need to be reminded of it. Relevant quotations will always help you to make your points more strongly.

F1 Do you agree that 'Portia is the most important character in the play'?

F2 Show how Shakespeare makes a contrast between Venice and Belmont.

F3 With detailed reference to the text of the play, describe the conflict between Antonio and Shylock.

F4 Describe *three* of Portia's suitors (other than Bassanio) and her attitudes towards them.

F5 In what ways is the sub-plot of Jessica and Lorenzo necessary to *The Merchant of Venice*?

F6 In Shakespeare's day, an alternative title for *The Merchant of Venice* was *The Jew of Venice*; which title do you think is the more appropriate?

G Projects

In some schools, students are asked to do more 'free-ranging' work, which takes them outside the text—but which should always be relevant to the play. Such Projects may demand skills other than reading and writing: design and artwork for instance, may be involved. Sometimes a 'portfolio' of work is assembled over a considerable period of time; and this can be presented to the examiner as part of the student's work for assessment.

The availability of resources will, obviously, do much to determine the nature of the Projects; but this is something that only the local teachers will understand. However, there is always help to be found in libraries, museums, and art galleries.

G1 Venice.

G2 Famous Actors and Actresses in *The Merchant of Venice*.

G3 Shakespeare's Theatre.

G4 Women in Shakespeare's England.

G5 Moneylenders.

Background

England c. 1599

When Shakespeare was writing *The Merchant of Venice*, most people still believed that the sun went round the earth. They were taught that this was a divinely ordered scheme of things, and that—in England—God had instituted a Church and ordained a Monarchy for the right government of the land and the populace.

'The past is a foreign country; they do things differently there.'

L. P. Hartley

Government For most of Shakespeare's life, the reigning monarch of England was Queen Elizabeth I. With her counsellors and ministers she governed the nation (population less than six million) from London, although fewer than half a million people inhabited the capital city. In the rest of the country, law and order were maintained by the land-owners and enforced by their deputies. The average man had no vote—and his wife had no rights at all.

Religion At this time, England was a Christian country. All children were baptized, soon after they were born, into the Church of England; they were taught the essentials of the Christian faith, and instructed in their duty to God and to humankind. Marriages were performed, and funerals conducted, only by the licensed clergy and in accordance with the Church's rites and ceremonies. Attendance at divine service was compulsory, and absences (without good—medical—reason) could be punished by fines. By such means, the authorities were able to keep some check on the populace—recording births, marriages, and deaths; being alert to any religious nonconformity, which could be politically dangerous; and ensuring a minimum of orthodox instruction through the official 'Homilies' which were regularly preached from the pulpits of all parish churches throughout the realm.

Following Henry VIII's break away from the Church of Rome, all people in England were able to hear the church services *in their own language*. The Book of Common Prayer was used in every church, and an English translation of the Bible was read aloud in public. The Christian religion had never been so well taught before!

Education School education reinforced the Church's teaching. From the age of four, boys might attend the 'petty school' (French '*petite école*') to learn the rudiments of reading and writing along with a few prayers; some schools also included work with numbers. At the age of seven, the boy was ready for the grammar school (if his father was willing and able to pay the fees).

Here, a thorough grounding in Latin grammar was followed by translation work and the study of Roman authors, paying attention as much to style as to matter. The arts of fine writing were thus inculcated from early youth. A very few students proceeded to university; these were either clever scholarship boys, or else the sons of noblemen. Girls stayed at home, and acquired domestic and social skills—cooking, sewing, perhaps even music. The lucky ones might learn to read and write.

Language At the start of the sixteenth century the English had a very poor opinion of their own language: there was little serious writing in English, and hardly any literature. Latin was the language of international scholarship, and Englishmen admired the eloquence of the Romans. They made many translations, and in this way they extended the resources of their own language, increasing its vocabulary and stretching its grammatical structures. French, Italian, and Spanish works were also translated and, for the first time, there were English versions of the Bible. By the end of the century, English was a language to be proud of: it was rich in synonyms, capable of infinite variety and subtlety, and ready for all kinds of word-play—especially the *puns*, for which Elizabethan English is renowned.

Drama The great art-form of the Elizabethan and Jacobean age was its drama. The Elizabethans inherited a tradition of play-acting from the Middle Ages, and they reinforced this by reading and translating the Roman playwrights. At the beginning of the sixteenth century plays were performed by groups of actors, all-male companies (boys acted the female roles) who travelled from town to town, setting up their stages in open places (such as inn-yards) or, with the permission of the owner, in the hall of some noble house. The touring companies continued in the provinces into the seventeenth century; but in London, in 1576, a new building was erected for the performance of plays. This was the Theatre, the first purpose-built playhouse in England. Other playhouses followed, (including the Globe, where most of Shakespeare's plays were performed), and the English drama reached new heights of eloquence.

There were those who disapproved, of course. The theatres, which brought large crowds together, could encourage the spread of disease—and dangerous ideas. During the summer, when the plague was at its worst, the playhouses were closed. A constant censorship was imposed, more or less severe at different times. The Puritan faction tried to close down the theatres, but—partly because there was royal favour for the drama, and partly because the buildings were outside the city limits—they did not succeed until 1642.

Theatre From contemporary comments and sketches—most particularly a drawing by a Dutch visitor, Johannes de Witt—it is possible to form some idea of the typical Elizabethan playhouse for which most of Shakespeare's plays were written. Hexagonal in shape, it had three roofed galleries encircling an open courtyard. The plain, high stage projected into the yard, where it was surrounded by the audience of standing 'groundlings'. At the back were two doors for the actors' entrances and exits, and between these doors was a curtained 'discovery space' (sometimes called an 'inner stage'). Above this was a balcony, used as a musicians' gallery or for the performance of scenes 'above'; and projecting over part of the stage was a roof, supported on two pillars, which was painted with the sun, moon, and stars for the 'heavens'.

Underneath was space (concealed by curtaining) which could be used by characters ascending and descending through a trap-door in the stage. Costumes and properties were kept backstage in the 'tiring house'. The actors dressed lavishly, often wearing the secondhand clothes bestowed by rich patrons. Stage properties were important for defining a location, but the dramatist's own words were needed to explain the time of day, since all performances took place in the early afternoon.

A replica of Shakespeare's own theatre, the Globe, has been built in London, and stands in Southwark, almost exactly on the Bankside site of the original.

Shakespeare's Globe, Southwark, London, England. Photograph by Richard Kalina.

Further Reading

Criticism:

Barnet, Sylvan (ed.), *Twentieth-century Interpretations of 'The Merchant of Venice'* (1970).
Brown, John Russell, *Shakespeare and His Comedies* (1957).
Granville-Barker, Harley, *Prefaces to Shakespeare, II* (1930).
Moody, A. D., *Shakespeare: 'The Merchant of Venice', Arnold Studies in English Literature* (1964).
Nevo, Ruth, *Comic Transformations in Shakespeare* (1980).
Stewart, Patrick, 'Shylock' in *Players of Shakespeare*, ed. Philip Brockbank (1985).
Vickers, Brian, *The Artistry of Shakespeare's Prose* (1968).
Wilders, John (ed.), *Shakespeare: 'The Merchant of Venice': A Casebook* (1969).

Sources:

Muir, Kenneth, *The Sources of Shakespeare's Plays* (London, 1977).

Additional Background Reading:

Bate, Jonathan, *The Genius of Shakespeare* (Picador [Macmillan], 1997).
Blake, N. F., *Shakespeare's Language: an Introduction* (London, 1983).
Gibson, Rex, *Shakespeare's Language* (Cambridge, 1997).
Honan, Park, *Shakespeare: A Life* (Oxford, 1998).
Langley, Andrew, *Shakespeare's Theatre* (Oxford, 1999).
Muir, K., and Schoenbaum, S., *A New Companion to Shakespeare Studies* (Cambridge, 1971).
Thomson, Peter, *Shakespeare's Theatre* (London, 1983).

William Shakespeare, 1564–1616

Elizabeth I was Queen of England when Shakespeare was born in 1564. He was the son of a tradesman who made and sold gloves in the small town of Stratford-upon-Avon, and he was educated at the grammar school in that town. Shakespeare did not go to university when he left school, but worked, perhaps, in his father's business. When he was eighteen he married Anne Hathaway, who became the mother of his daughter, Susanna, in 1583, and of twins in 1585.

There is nothing exciting, or even unusual, in this story; and from 1585 until 1592 there are no documents that can tell us anything at all about Shakespeare. But we have learned that in 1592 he was known in London, and that he had become both an actor and a playwright.

We do not know when Shakespeare wrote his first play, and indeed we are not sure of the order in which he wrote his works. If you look on page 119 at the list of his writings and their approximate dates, you will see how he started by writing plays on subjects taken from the history of England. No doubt this was partly because he was always an intensely patriotic man—but he was also a very shrewd business-man. He could see that the theatre audiences enjoyed being shown their own history, and it was certain that he would make a profit from this kind of drama.

The plays in the next group are mainly comedies, with romantic love-stories of young people who fall in love with one another, and at the end of the play marry and live happily ever after.

At the end of the sixteenth century the happiness disappears, and Shakespeare's plays become melancholy, bitter, and tragic. This change may have been caused by some sadness in the writer's life (one of his twins died in 1596). Shakespeare, however, was not the only writer whose works at this time were very serious. The whole of England was facing a crisis. Queen Elizabeth I was growing old. She was greatly loved, and the people were sad to think she must soon die; they were also afraid, for the queen had never married, and so there was no child to succeed her.

When James I came to the throne in 1603, Shakespeare continued to write serious drama—the great tragedies and the plays based on Roman history for which he is most famous. Finally, before he retired from the theatre, he wrote another set of comedies. These all have the same theme: they tell of happiness which is lost, and then found again.

Shakespeare returned from London to Stratford, his home town. He was rich and successful, and he owned one of the biggest houses in the town. He died in 1616.

Shakespeare also wrote two long poems, and a collection of sonnets. The sonnets describe two love-affairs, but we do not know who the lovers were. Although there are many public documents concerned with his career as a writer and a business-man, Shakespeare has hidden his personal life from us. A nineteenth-century poet, Matthew Arnold, addressed Shakespeare in a poem, and wrote 'We ask and ask—Thou smilest, and art still'.

There is not even a trustworthy portrait of the world's greatest dramatist.

Approximate order of composition of Shakespeare's works

Period	Comedies	History plays	Tragedies	Poems
I	Comedy of Errors	Henry VI, part 1	Titus Andronicus	
	Taming of the Shrew	Henry VI, part 2		
1594	Two Gentlemen of Verona	Henry VI, part 3		
		Richard III		Venus and Adonis
	Love's Labour's Lost	King John		Rape of Lucrece
II	Midsummer Night's Dream	Richard II	Romeo and Juliet	
	Merchant of Venice	Henry IV, part 1		
1599	Merry Wives of Windsor	Henry IV, part 2		
	Much Ado About Nothing			
	As You Like It	Henry V		Sonnets
III	Twelfth Night		Julius Caesar	
	Troilus and Cressida		Hamlet	
1608	Measure for Measure		Othello	
	All's Well That Ends Well		Timon of Athens	
			King Lear	
			Macbeth	
			Antony and Cleopatra	
			Coriolanus	
IV	Pericles			
	Cymbeline			
1613	The Winter's Tale			
	The Tempest	Henry VIII